CLASSICS AT HOME

SECTION I

PETER RABBIT & FRIENDS

STUDY GUIDE:

A Guide for Children
for the Works of
Beatrix Potter

by Ann Ward

NOBLE PUBLISHING ASSOCIATES
GRESHAM, OREGON

NOBLE PUBLISHING ASSOCIATES

Noble Publishing Associates is an association of Christian authors dedicated to serving God and assisting one another in the production, promotion, and distribution of audio, video, and print publications. For instructions on how you may participate in our association, or for information about our complete line of materials, write to:

Noble Publishing Associates
P.O. Box 2250
Gresham, Oregon 97030

or call **(503) 667-3942.**

IMPORTANT NOTE: The page numbers listed in this book were taken from:

- **The complete Tales of Beatrix Potter** by Beatrix Potter
  Warne Publishers, ISBN 0-7232-3618-6
- **The House at Pooh Corner** by A.A. Milne
  Dutton Publishers, ISBN 0-525-44444-0
- **Winnie-the-Pooh** by A.A. Milne
  Dutton Publishers, ISBN 0-525-44443-2

Third Printing, 1996

ISBN: 0-923463-96-8

Printed in the United States of America

TABLE OF CONTENTS

Section I: Peter Rabbit & Friends

SECTION II: CHARLOTTE & WINNIE

A Note to Parents

This Study Guide is designed to present an organized way to study the works of Beatrix Potter. It is one in a series of Classics At Home Study Guides to help expose children to some of the finest classics in children's literature.

Beatrix Potter not only presented good story lines and marvelous vocabulary, but also accurate drawings of the animals she wrote about, in wonderful watercolor illustrations. Some of the vocabulary lists are lengthy, and I have been tempted to shorten them; but I know that children are fascinated with long words. If the new words are presented with enthusiasm on your part as an exciting adventure to learn more precise ways of describing things - a game, I know you will be amazed at your little ones using these words in daily life!

Depending on the reading ability and dictionary skills of your child, you may want to go through the vocabulary lists with your child. Before having him/her begin using the Guide, make sure your child understands that a complete sentence is one complete thought. It begins with a capital letter and ends with a period (or ? or !). There is at least one naming word (pronoun or noun) and one action word (verb).

This Guide is meant to be "non-consumable" (not used up with each use; not written in). I suggest that you have your child begin a notebook section for this study - and have the answer sheets (answers written on notebook paper), drawings, and sheets with information on various topics of further study added to the notebook.

One of the activities for each book is to "read the story to a younger child." This will, hopefully, add more fluency in reading (after having learned the vocabulary words) and allow your younger children to hear a good story.

Enjoy your child's visits with Peter Rabbit, Mrs. Tiggy–winkle, Jemima Puddleduck, Mr. Jeremy Fisher, and all the others. Hopefully, this study will help your child gain an appreciation for excellent literature, a fine choice of words, beautiful art, and the wonder of some of God's creations.

LET'S LEARN ABOUT THE AUTHORS

Beatrix Potter grew up in the city of London, England, and spent each summer in the country. As a small girl, she loved studying animals and plants. She also loved to draw. Beatrix's first governess, a woman who taught her at home, was Miss Hammond. She taught Beatrix to carefully observe animals and plants. She encouraged Beatrix to draw from real models instead of copying drawings from books.

Beatrix did not go to a school outside of her home. She learned by observing and studying by herself. She was glad she could study at home. Miss Annie Carter came when Beatrix was sixteen, to teach her the German language. Later, Miss Carter married a man named Mr. Moore and had a son, Noel. Beatrix once wrote to Noel when he was sick. She made up a story about a rabbit named Peter and his adventures in Mr. McGregor's garden. She later wrote many other stories to Annie's children.

Beatrix Potter's books have been translated into many different languages. Children from around the world have loved the familiar characters of Peter Rabbit, Benjamin Bunny, Mrs. Tiggy-winkle, Jemima, Puddle-Duck, and all the rest.

A.A. Milne was born in 1882 in London, England. He was a playwright and journalist as well as a poet and storyteller. Winnie-the-Pooh, The House At Pooh Corner, When We Were Very Young and Now We are Six were inspired by his son, Christopher Robin.

A.A. Milne died in 1956.

FIND OUT WHAT THESE WORDS MEAN:

1. hedgehog
2. observe
3. specimen
4. journal
5. publishers
6. illustrated
7. purchased
8. village
9. sheepherding
10. adjoining
11. naturalist
12. translated
13. characters

PLEASE ANSWER THESE IN COMPLETE SENTENCES:

14. As a child, what did Beatrix Potter love to do?

15. Name at least two pets that Beatrix Potter had.

16. Where did Beatrix Potter go to school?

17. While she and her family went to the country in the summers, what did Beatrix do?

18. What story did Beatrix Potter make up for Noel Moore when he was sick once?

19. How many publishers did Beatrix try for her Peter Rabbit book—and what did they say?

20. What did Beatrix Potter decide to do with her Peter Rabbit story?

21. Where did Beatrix enjoy being?

22. Name the two farms that Beatrix purchased.

23. Name three things that Beatrix Potter did well.

LEARNING MORE:

24. Find England on a map or globe. Then find the city of London.

25. Learn more about pressing flowers and leaves. Try it yourself.

26. Begin keeping a journal—writing each day about what is happening in your life.

27. Begin studying animals, bugs, flowers, plants, and trees. Think about the special features God has given each. Draw each specimen you observe. Try to label each and show its special features.

THE STORY OF A FIERCE BAD RABBIT

❑ **READ** <u>**The Story of A Fierce Bad Rabbit.**</u> (p. 131)

🐝 **FIND OUT WHAT THESE WORDS MEAN:**
1. savage (p. 133)
2. gentle (p. 133)
3. rushes up (p. 138)
4. peeps (p. 138)
5. tearing (p. 138)

✏️ **PLEASE ANSWER THESE IN COMPLETE SENTENCES:**
6. How were the two rabbits different?
7. How did the fierce bad rabbit get the carrot?
8. What did the good rabbit do then?
9. After the hunter shot, what did he find left on the bench?
10. What lesson can you learn from the story?

✔ **LEARNING MORE:**
11. Read Galatians 6:7 (ask your parents for help in finding it in the Bible). How does this apply to the story?
12. Draw a picture of your favorite part of this story.
13. Which is your favorite illustration from the story—and why?
14. Read this story to a younger child.
15. Make up sentences using at least two of the vocabulary words.

APPLEY DAPPLY'S NURSERY RHYMES

❑ **READ** <u>Appley Dapply's Nursery Rhymes.</u> (p. 309)

❧ **FIND OUT WHAT THESE WORDS MEAN:**
1. charming (p. 311)
2. sharp (p. 312)
3. fond (p. 312)
4. (pin) cushion (p. 314)
5. surely (p. 314)
6. velvet (p. 315)
7. delves (p. 315)
8. amiable (p. 316)
9. guinea-pig (p. 316)
10. periwig (p. 316)

✎ **PLEASE ANSWER THESE IN COMPLETE SENTENCES:**
11. Name four of the six different animals shown in the story.
12. Which is the animal shown on page 314?
13. What type of pins is the author talking about on page 314?

✔ **LEARNING MORE:**
14. Find out more about guinea-pigs. In the Reading section of your notebook, write about what you have learned.
15. Find out more about moles. In the Reading section of your notebook, write about what you have learned.
16. Memorize your favorite rhyme from the chapter.
17. Draw an illustration of your favorite part of the chapter.
18. Read this chapter of rhymes to a younger child.
19. Make up sentences using at least four of the vocabulary words.

CECILY PARSLEY'S NURSERY RHYMES

❏ **READ** <u>Cecily Parsley's Nursery Rhymes</u>. (p. 331)

❦ **FIND OUT WHAT THESE WORDS MEAN:**
1. pen (p. 333)
2. brewed (p. 333)
3. ale (p. 333)
4. gentlemen (p. 333)
5. gander (p. 334)
6. whither (p. 334)
7. chamber (p. 334)
8. market (p. 334)
9. fair (p. 336)
10. fare (p. 336)
11. carving (p. 337)
12. sown (p. 338)
13. tend (p. 338)
14. faded (p. 338)
15. blighted (p. 338)
16. blossom (p. 338)
17. petticoat (p. 338)

✎ **PLEASE ANSWER THESE IN COMPLETE SENTENCES:**
18. Name six of the nine kinds of animals shown in the illustrations.
19. What does the sign "To Let" on page 333 mean?
20. What is the answer to the riddle on page 338?

✔ **LEARNING MORE:**
21. Memorize your favorite rhyme from this collection.
22. Draw an illustration of your favorite part of the chapter.
23. Read this chapter of rhymes to a younger child.
24. Make up sentences using at least seven of the vocabulary words.

THE STORY OF MISS MOPPET

❏ **READ** **The Story of Miss Moppet.** (p. 139)

❦ **FIND OUT WHAT THESE WORDS MEAN:**

1. duster (p. 143)

2. bell-pull (p. 143)

3. all of a sudden (p. 144)

4. teased (p. 144)

5. wriggled (p. 146)

6. jig (p. 146)

✐ **PLEASE ANSWER THESE IN COMPLETE SENTENCES:**

7. What color bow does Miss Moppet wear?

8. After Miss Moppet missed catching the mouse on the first try, what was her next plan?

9. What did Miss Moppet do with the mouse after she caught him?

10. What was the end result of the story?

✔ **LEARNING MORE:**

11. Draw four pictures to tell the story of Miss Moppet. Give it to a young child.

12. Which was your favorite illustration from the story? What did you like about it?

13. Read this story to a younger child.

14. Make up sentences using at least three of the vocabulary words.

The Tale of Peter Rabbit

Part I

☐ **READ PAGES 9-15 IN <u>The Tale of Peter Rabbit</u>.**

❧ **FIND OUT WHAT THESE WORDS MEAN:**
1. mischief (p. 11)
2. wood (p. 12)
3. currant (p. 12)
4. naughty (p. 12)
5. dreadfully (p. 15)
6. unfortunately (p. 15)
7. gooseberry (p. 15)
8. shed (p. 15)
9. sobs (p. 15)
10. overheard (p. 15)
11. implored (p. 15)
12. exert (p. 15)

✎ **PLEASE ANSWER THESE IN COMPLETE SENTENCES:**
13. What were the four little rabbits' names?
14. What had happened to Peter's father?
15. Where did Mrs. Rabbit go?
16. What instructions did she tell her children?
17. What did each of the rabbit children do after their mother left?
18. What did Peter eat in Mr. McGregor's garden?
19. Where did Peter get caught?

✔ **LEARNING MORE:**
20. Find out what a cucumber frame is.
21. Find out what gooseberries and currants look like. In the Reading section of your note
    book, write about what you have learned.
22. Plant some pea or bean seeds and watch them grow. (You may try planting them in a
    glass—near the edge so you can watch the plant develop.)
23. Draw a picture of your favorite part of the story so far.
24. Make up sentences using at least seven of the vocabulary words.

The Tale of Peter Rabbit

Part II

❏ **READ PAGES 16-20 IN <u>The Tale of Peter Rabbit</u>.**

❧ **FIND OUT WHAT THESE WORDS MEAN:**
1. sieve (p. 16)
2. wriggled (p. 16)
3. rushed (p. 16)
4. upsetting (p. 17)
5. trembling (p. 17)
6. least (p. 17)
7. damp (p. 17)
8. doorstep (p. 17)
9. puzzled (p. 18)
10. twitched (p. 18)
11. scuttered (p. 18)
12. presently (p. 18)
13. peeped (p. 18)
14. fortnight (p. 20)
15. camomile (p. 20)
16. dose (p. 20)

✐ **PLEASE ANSWER THESE IN COMPLETE SENTENCES:**
17. What animals did Peter see in the garden?
18. Where did Peter hide from Mr. McGregor?
19. Who was Peter's cousin?
20. What noise did the hoe make?
21. Name at least five crops Mr. McGregor grew in his garden.
22. What did Mr. McGregor do with Peter's jacket?
23. What did Peter's mother give him in bed?
24. What did Peter's obedient brother and sisters get to eat for dinner?
25. If you had a garden, how would you feel about animals chewing up your food crops?

✔ **LEARNING MORE:**
26. Learn more about rabbits from the encyclopedia or another book. In the Reading section of your notebook, write about what you have learned.
27. Draw a picture of your favorite part of this section of the story.
28. Read the story to a younger child—OR act it out with puppets.
29. Make up sentences using at least seven of the vocabulary words.

THE TALE OF TWO BAD MICE

Part I

☐ **READ PAGES 69-77 IN <u>The Tale of Two Bad Mice</u>.**

❧ **FIND OUT WHAT THESE WORDS MEAN:**

1. muslin (p. 71)
2. shavings (p. 71)
3. perambulator (p. 72)
4. scuffling (p. 72)
5. skirting-board (p. 72)
6. oilcloth (p. 73)
7. coalbox (p. 73)
8. cautiously (p. 73)
9. hearthrug (p. 73)
10. fast (p. 73)
11. lead (p. 74)
12. convenient (p. 74)
13. carve (p. 74)
14. streaked (p. 74)
15. crumpled (p. 74)
16. cheesemonger's (p. 75)
17. jerk (p. 75)
18. temper (p. 76)
19. shiny (p. 76)
20. plaster (p. 76)
21. rage (p. 77)
22. disappointment (p. 77)
23. crinkly (p. 77)
24. soot (p. 77)

✐ **PLEASE ANSWER THESE IN COMPLETE SENTENCES:**

25. What did the dollhouse look like?
26. To whom did the dollhouse belong?
27. Name at least three of the pretend foods in the dollhouse.
28. What were the names of the two mice who visited the dollhouse?
29. What was the first room the mice explored?
30. Why could the mice not cut the food?
31. What was Tom Thumb feeling and how did he show his feelings?

✔ **LEARNING MORE:**

32. Draw and color or paint a picture of your favorite part of the story so far.
33. From the encyclopedia or other book, learn more about mice. In the Reading section of your notebook, write about what you have learned.
34. Make up sentences using at least ten of the vocabulary words.

15

THE TALE OF TWO BAD MICE

Part II

☐ **READ PAGES 78-84 IN <u>The Tale of Two Bad Mice</u>.**

❦ **FIND OUT WHAT THESE WORDS MEAN:**
1. canisters (p. 78)
2. Sago (p. 78)
3. chest of drawers (p. 78)
4. frugal (p. 79)
5. bolster (p. 79)
6. in want of (p. 79)
7. assistance (p. 79)
8. managed (p. 79)
9. cradle (p. 80)
10. suddenly (p. 80)
11. landing (p. 80)
12. sight (p. 81)
13. upset (p. 81)
14. remark (p. 81)
15. rescued (p. 81)

✎ **PLEASE ANSWER THESE IN COMPLETE SENTENCES:**
19. What did Hunca Munca do while Tom Thumb was up the chimney?
20. What did the mice do with the bolster?
21. Name three other items that the mice took from the dollhouse?
22. What did the dolls do when they returned to their house?
23. What was the nurse's comment about solving the "mouse problem"?
24. What two things did Tom Thumb and Hunca Munca do for Lucinda and Jane?
25. What lesson can we learn from this story?

✔ **LEARNING MORE:**
26. Draw a picture of your favorite part of this section of the story.
27. Read the story to a younger child—OR make a series of pictures that tell the story in order.
28. Make up sentences using at least seven of the vocabulary words.

THE TALE OF TOM KITTEN

Part I

☐ **READ PAGES 147-154a IN <u>The Tale of Tom Kitten</u>.**

🐁 **FIND OUT WHAT THESE WORDS MEAN:**

1. tumbled (p. 149)
2. expected (p. 149)
3. to tea (p. 149)
4. fetched (p. 149)
5. fine (p. 149)
6. arrived (p. 149)
7. pinafores (p. 151)
8. tuckers (p. 151)
9. elegant (p. 151)
10. uncomfortable (p. 151)
11. burst (p. 151)
12. unwisely (p. 151)
13. turned them out (p. 151)
14. frocks (p. 151)
15. hind (p. 152)
16. ash-pit (p. 152)
17. pigsty (p. 152)
18. path (p. 152)
19. unsteadily (p. 152)
20. trod (p. 152)
21. several (p. 152)
22. smears (p. 152)
23. rockery (p. 153)
24. trousers (p. 153)
25. by degrees (p. 153)
26. shedding (p. 153)
27. right and left (p. 153)
28. in difficulties (p. 154)
29. goose step (p. 154)
30. waddle (p. 154)

✏️ **PLEASE ANSWER THESE IN COMPLETE SENTENCES:**

31. What were Mrs. Tabitha Twitchit's children named?
32. How did Tom behave while he was being cleaned up?
33. Why did Mrs. Twitchit want the children to get all dressed up?
34. Does God want us to be concerned about clothes and impressing others?
35. Where did Mrs. Tabitha Twitchit send her children before the company arrived?
36. What color were Tom's clothes?
37. Name one flower or animal you recognized in the garden (besides the kittens).
38. Onto what did the three kittens climb?
39. What happened to Tom's clothes as he tried to climb the wall?

✔ **LEARNING MORE:**

40. In the encyclopedia or another book about animals, find out more about cats and kittens.
41. Draw a picture of your favorite part of this section of the story.
42. Make up sentences using at least ten of the vocabulary words.

THE TALE OF TOM KITTEN

Part II

❑ **READ PAGES 154b-158 IN <u>The Tale of Tom Kitten</u>.**

🍎 **FIND OUT WHAT THESE WORDS MEAN:**

1. row (p. 154)
2. stared (p. 154)
3. descended (p. 155)
4. advanced (p. 155)
5. sideways (p. 155)
6. manner (p. 155)
7. various (p. 155)
8. articles (p. 155)
9. not fit to be seen (p. 157)
10. affronted (p. 157)
11. measles (p. 157)
12. quite the contrary (p. 157)
13. extraordinary (p. 157)
14. overhead (p. 157)
15. disturbed (p. 157)
16. dignity (p. 157)
17. repose (p. 157)
18. directly (p. 158)

✏️ **PLEASE ANSWER THESE IN COMPLETE SENTENCES:**

19. What were the names of the three animals that walked on the road?
20. What happened to the kittens' clothing?
21. What did Mrs. Tabitha Twitchit do with the kittens when she saw them on the wall?
22. Why was she upset with the kittens?
23. What did Mrs. Twitchit tell her friends about the kittens?
24. What mischief did the kittens get into while their mother was having her tea party?
25. How did it affect the tea party?
26. What happened to the Puddle-Ducks' clothes in the pond?
27. What explanation does Beatrix Potter give for why ducks put their heads under the water and their tails up in the air?
28. What lessons can we learn from this story?
29. What good (and bad) characteristics did Mrs. Tabitha Twitchit have?

✔ **LEARNING MORE:**

30. Learn more about ducks from the encyclopedia or another book. In the Reading section of your notebook, write about what you have learned. Find out the real reason they put their heads under water.
31. Draw a picture of your favorite part of this section of the story.
32. Read this story to a younger child.
33. Make up sentences using at least nine of the vocabulary words.

THE TALE OF MR. JEREMY FISHER

Part I

❑ **READ PAGES 119-125 IN <u>The Tale of Mr. Jeremy Fisher</u>.**

🍎 **FIND OUT WHAT THESE WORDS MEAN:**

1. damp (p. 121)
2. amongst (p. 121)
3. buttercups (p. 121)
4. edge (p. 121)
5. larder (p. 121)
6. passage (p. 121)
7. scolded (p. 121)
8. minnows (p. 122)
9. tortoise (p. 122)
10. bait (p. 122-illustration)
11. macintosh (p. 122)
12. galoshes (p. 122)
13. rod (p. 122)
14. enormous (p. 122)
15. reed (p. 123)
16. tackle (p. 123)
17. stalk (p. 123)
18. trickled (p. 123)
19. tiresome (p. 123)
20. punted (p. 124)
21. shower (p. 124)
22. lily (p. 125)
23. tweaked (p. 125)
24. rushes (p. 125)
25. directly (p. 125)
26. float (p. 125)
27. jerking (p. 125)

✏️ **PLEASE ANSWER THESE IN COMPLETE SENTENCES:**

28. Name the creature on the larder wall on page 121.
29. Describe the clothes that Mr. Jeremy Fisher wore.
30. What did Jeremy use for a boat?
31. What did Jeremy use for a fishing line?
32. What nibbled on Jeremy's shoe while he was eating his sandwich?

✔ **LEARNING MORE:**

33. Learn more about fishing. In the Reading section of your notebook, write about what you have learned.
34. A tortoise is a kind of turtle. Learn more about tortoises and other kinds of turtles. In the Reading section of your notebook, write about what you have learned.
35. Draw a picture of your favorite part so far in the story.
36. Make up sentences using at least ten of the vocabulary words.

THE TALE OF MR. JEREMY FISHER

Part II

☐ **READ PAGES 126-130 IN <u>The Tale of Mr. Jeremy Fisher</u>.**

❧ **FIND OUT WHAT THESE WORDS MEAN:**

1. stickleback (p. 126)
2. spines (p. 126)
3. floundered (p. 126)
4. snapping (p. 126)
5. shoal (p. 126)
6. disconsolately (p. 127)
7. seized (p. 127)
8. dived (p. 127)
9. displeased (p. 127)
10. spat (p. 127)
11. cork (p. 128)
12. scrambled (p. 128)
13. bank (p. 128)
14. meadow (p. 128)
15. tatters (p. 128)
16. pike (p. 128)
17. sticking plaster (p. 129)
18. offer (p. 129)
19. waistcoat (p. 129)
20. nasty (p. 130)

✎ **PLEASE ANSWER THESE IN COMPLETE SENTENCES:**

21. What did Jeremy catch on his line instead of a minnow?
22. How did Jeremy feel about this catch?
23. What terrible thing happened as he sat on his boat then?
24. What saved Jeremy from being swallowed by the trout?
25. In what condition was Jeremy's coat as he hopped home?
26. Who came to dinner?
27. What did Jeremy serve his guests?

✔ **LEARNING MORE:**

28. What was your favorite illustration in the story? What in particular did you like about it?
29. Draw and color or paint a picture of your favorite part of this part of the story.
30. Learn more about worms or newts. In the Reading section of your notebook, write about what you have learned.
31. Learn more about water lilies. In the Reading section of your notebook, write about what you have learned.
32. Read this story to a younger child.
33. Make up sentences using at least ten of the vocabulary words.

THE TALE OF SQUIRREL NUTKIN

Part I

☐ **READ PAGES 21-29 IN <u>The Tale of Squirrel Nutkin</u>.**

❧ **FIND OUT WHAT THESE WORDS MEAN:**

1. island (p. 23)
2. ripe (p. 24)
3. hazel (p. 24)
4. rafts (p. 24)
5. paddled (p. 24)
6. gather (p. 24)
7. oar (p. 24)
8. offering (p. 25)
9. bow (p. 25)
10. politely (p. 25)
11. favour, (favor) (p. 25)
12. permission (p. 25)
13. excessively (p. 25)
14. impertinent (p. 25)
15. manners (p. 25)
16. bobbed (p. 25)
17. groat (p. 25)
18. riddle (p. 25)
19. "as old as the hills" (p. 25)
20. obstinately (p. 25)
21. gracious (p. 27)
22. respect (p. 27)
23. nettle (p. 27)
24. thread (p. 28)
25. oak-apples (p. 28)
26. scarlet (p. 28)
27. landed (p. 29)
28. crooked (p. 29)

✎ **PLEASE ANSWER THESE IN COMPLETE SENTENCES:**

29. What was the main character's name?
30. Who was his brother?
31. How did the squirrels make rafts?
32. What did the squirrels use for sails?
33. What was in the center of the lake? Who lived there? What was his name?
34. Name the offerings the squirrels brought to Mr. Brown the first three mornings.
35. What did Nutkin do to Mr. Brown each morning?
36. How did Mr. Brown react?
37. While the other squirrels gathered nuts the second morning, what did Nutkin do?

✔ **LEARNING MORE:**

38. Which was your favorite illustration from this section of the story? Why?
39. Draw a picture of your favorite part of the story so far.
40. Learn more about islands. In the Reading section of your notebook, write about what you have learned.
41. Learn more about squirrels. In the Reading section of your notebook, write about what you have learned.
42. Make up sentences using at least ten of the vocabulary words.

THE TALE OF SQUIRREL NUTKIN

Part II

❏ **READ PAGES 30-36 IN <u>The Tale of Squirrel Nutkin</u>.**

❦ **FIND OUT WHAT THESE WORDS MEAN:**

1. plum-pudding (p. 30)
2. dock-leaf (p. 30)
3. rudely (p. 30)
4. ridiculous (p. 30)
5. briar (p. 30)
6. tippitty top (p. 31)
7. flock (p. 31)
8. bonny (p. 31)
9. swine (p. 31)
10. disgust (p. 31)
11. crab apple (p. 32)
12. ninepins (p. 32)
13. rush (p. 32)
14. parting (p. 32)
15. beck (p. 32)
16. counterpane (p. 32)
17. wrights (p. 32)
18. whirring (p. 34)
19. flutterment (p. 34)
20. scufflement (p. 34)
21. scuttered (p. 34)
22. cautiously (p. 34)
23. intending (p. 35)
24. skin (p. 35)
25. dashed (p. 35)
26. staircase (p. 35)
27. attic (p. 35)

✏ **PLEASE ANSWER THESE IN COMPLETE SENTENCES:**

28. What gifts did the squirrels bring to Mr. Brown on the fourth, fifth and sixth days?
29. How did Mr. Brown respond to the presents?
30. While the other squirrels gathered nuts on the fourth day, what did Nutkin do?
31. What did Nutkin do to Mr. Brown on the sixth day after the egg was given as a gift?
32. What did the owl do to Nutkin on the doorstep?
33. What did Mr. Brown do to Nutkin inside his house?
34. How did Nutkin escape?
35. What did Nutkin leave behind?
36. According to the story, how would Nutkin react if you were to ask him a riddle?

✔ **LEARNING MORE:**

37. Which was your favorite illustration from this section of the story? Why?
38. Draw a picture of your favorite part of today's reading.
39. Learn more about owls. In the Reading section of your notebook, write about what you have learned.
40. Learn some riddles. Tell them to your family.
41. Read this story to a younger child.
42. Make up sentences using at least ten of the vocabulary words.

THE TALE OF BENJAMIN BUNNY

Part I

❑ **READ PAGES 53-61 IN <u>The Tale of Benjamin Bunny</u>.**

❧ **FIND OUT WHAT THESE WORDS MEAN:**

1. pricked (p. 55)
2. trot (p. 55)
3. gig (p. 55)
4. relations (p. 55)
5. widow (p. 56)
6. muffetees (p. 56)
7. herbs (p. 56)
8. bazaar (p. 56)
9. rosemary (p. 56)
10. tumbled (p. 56)
11. poorly (p. 56)
12. assured (p. 58)
13. fetch (p. 58)
14. camomile (p. 58)
15. plainly (p. 59)
16. tam-o-shanter (p. 59)
17. consequence (p. 59)
18. clogs (p. 60)
19. shrunk (p. 60)
20. suggested (p. 61)
21. contrary (p. 61)
22. habit (p. 61)

✎ **PLEASE ANSWER THESE IN COMPLETE SENTENCES:**

23. Who did Benjamin Bunny see driving down the road one morning?
24. Who were Benjamin's relatives?
25. Who did Benjamin find as he walked toward his aunt's home?
26. What was Peter wearing—and why?
27. Where did the two cousins go?
28. How did they enter the garden?
29. Why did Benjamin want to get Peter's clothes back first?
30. What did Benjamin begin putting in the handkerchief—and why?
31. How did each of the rabbits feel about being in the garden?
32. Did Benjamin come to the garden often?
33. What was the name of Benjamin's dad?

✔ **LEARNING MORE:**

34. Learn more about herbs (for example: lavender, camomile, rosemary). In the Reading section of your notebook, write about what you have learned.
35. Which is your favorite illustration from this part of the story—and why?
36. Draw a picture of your favorite part of this section of the story.
37. Make up sentences using at least ten of the vocabulary words.

THE TALE OF BENJAMIN BUNNY

Part II

☐ **READ PAGES 62-68 IN <u>The Tale of Benjamin Bunny</u>.**

❧ **FIND OUT WHAT THESE WORDS MEAN:**

1. boldly (p. 62)
2. planks (p. 62)
3. cherry stones (p. 62)
4. winked (p. 62)
5. at length (p. 65)
6. mortar (p. 65)
7. prancing (p. 65)
8. terrace (p. 65)
9. switch (p. 65)
10. no opinion (p. 66)
11. tremendous (p. 66)
12. cuffed (p. 66)
13. nephew (p. 66)
14. marched (p. 67)
15. perplexed (p. 67)
16. ridiculously (p. 67)

✏ **PLEASE ANSWER THESE IN COMPLETE SENTENCES:**

17. How many times did Peter drop the load of onions?
18. What did Peter and Benjamin see around the corner of the greenhouse?
19. Where did Benjamin hide them?
20. What color bow did the cat have on?
21. How long did the cat stay on top of the basket?
22. What did Mr. Benjamin Bunny have in his hand—and why?
23. What did Mr. Bunny do when he saw the cat on top of the basket?
24. What did Mr. Bunny do with the cat?
25. How did the cat react to this?
26. What did Mr. Bunny do with the two rabbit boys?
27. What did Mr. Bunny carry out of the garden besides the handkerchief of onions?
28. Look at the difference between the rabbits' ears on pages 43 and 55. Describe the different feelings they were probably having.
29. What two things puzzled Mr. McGregor when he returned home?
30. How did Mrs. Rabbit feel toward Peter when he returned home?

✔ **LEARNING MORE:**

31. Which was your favorite illustration from this part of the story? Why?
32. Draw a picture showing your favorite part of this section of the story.
33. Read this story to a younger child.
34. Make up sentences using at least ten of the vocabulary words.

THE TALE OF THE FLOPSY BUNNIES

Part I

☐ **READ PAGES 197-203a IN** <u>The Tale of The Flopsy Bunnies</u>.

🍎 **FIND OUT WHAT THESE WORDS MEAN:**

1. soporific (p. 199)
2. improvident (p. 199)
3. rubbish (p. 200)
4. ditch (p. 200)
5. mowing machine (p. 200)
6. marrows (p. 200)
7. quantity (p. 200)
8. overgrown (p. 200)
9. shot (p. 200)
10. by degrees (p. 201)
11. overcome (p. 201)
12. slumber (p. 201)
13. mown (p. 201)
14. sufficiently (p. 201)
15. delightfully (p. 201)
16. blue-bottles (p. 201)
17. apologized (p. 201)
18. profusely (p. 201)
19. tread (p. 202)
20. shrank (p. 202)
21. stirred (p. 203)

✏️ **PLEASE ANSWER THESE IN COMPLETE SENTENCES:**

22. Who did Benjamin Bunny marry?
23. What did Peter do when he "grew up"?
24. What were two sources of food for the Benjamin Bunny family?
25. What did the Flopsy Bunnies eat in the rubbish heap?
26. What happened to them as a result of eating that?
27. What was the woodmouse's name?
28. What did Thomasina and Benjamin do when Mr. McGregor dumped the cloppings from overhead?
29. What did Mr. McGregor notice sticking up through the lawn clippings?
30. How many bunnies did Mr. McGregor put into the sack?
31. What color jacket did Benjamin wear?

✔ **LEARNING MORE:**

32. Which was your favorite illustration from this part of the story—and why?
33. Draw a picture of your favorite part of this section of the story.
34. Make up sentences using at least ten of the vocabulary words.

THE TALE OF THE FLOPSY BUNNIES

Part II

❑ **READ PAGES 203b-208 IN <u>The Tale of The Flopsy Bunnies</u>.**

🐛 **FIND OUT WHAT THESE WORDS MEAN:**

1. remained (p. 203)
2. suspiciously (p. 203)
3. doleful (p. 204)
4. despair (p. 204)
5. undo (p. 204)
6. resourceful (p. 204)
7. blacking-brush (p. 204)
8. decayed (p. 204)
9. crept (p. 205)
10. extremely (p. 205)
11. flags (p. 206)
12. chuckle (p. 206)
13. enquired (p. 206)
14. cloak (p. 206)
15. hood (p. 208)
16. handsome (p. 208)
17. muff (p. 208)

✏️ **PLEASE ANSWER THESE IN COMPLETE SENTENCES:**

18. How did Thomasina rescue the bunnies?

19. What did the rabbit parents put in the sack as replacements for the bunnies?

20. What did Mr. McGregor and Mrs. McGregor each want to do with the rabbit skins?

21. What did Mrs. McGregor do after she felt the vegetables inside the bag?

22. What did the Flopsy Bunnies do for Mrs. Tittlemouse?

23. How does the saying "Don't count your chickens before they are hatched" apply to this story?

✔ **LEARNING MORE:**

24. What illustration from this section was your favorite—and why?

25. Draw a picture of your favorite scene from this section of the story.

26. Read this story to a younger child.

27. Make up sentences using at least seven of the vocabulary words.

THE TALE OF MRS. TITTLEMOUSE

Part I

☐ **READ PAGES 223-229 IN <u>The Tale of Mrs. Tittlemouse</u>.**

🐛 **FIND OUT WHAT THESE WORDS MEAN:**

1. hedge (p. 225)
2. sandy (p. 225)
3. passages (p. 225)
4. storerooms (p. 225)
5. parlour (p. 225)
6. pantry (p. 225)
7. larder (p. 225)
8. terribly (p. 226)
9. tidy (p. 226)
10. particular (p. 226)
11. clattering (p. 226)
12. spotty (p. 226)
13. cloak (p. 226)
14. shelter (p. 226)
15. bold (p. 226)
16. bundled (p. 227)
17. distant (p. 227)
18. fetch (p. 227)
19. thistle-down (p. 227)
20. cowslips (p. 227)
21. severely (p. 227)
22. beeswax (p. 227)
23. cross (p. 228)
24. peevish (p. 228)
25. sidled (p. 228)
26. untidy (p. 228)
27. moss (p. 228)
28. letting (p. 228)
29. lodgings (p. 228)
30. intrusion (p. 228)
31. twiddling (p. 229)
32. fender (p. 229)
33. drain (p. 229)
34. coat tails (p. 229)

✏ **PLEASE ANSWER THESE IN COMPLETE SENTENCES:**

35. Describe what Mrs. Tittlemouse's house looked like.
36. Name at least four of the seven kinds of unexpected visitors Mrs. Tittlemouse had.
37. How did she feel about the visitors?
38. Why had Mr. Jackson come?
39. Was he very considerate of Mrs. Tittlemouse's desire for a clean home?

✔ **LEARNING MORE:**

40. Learn more about bees and honey. In the Reading section of your notebook, write about what you have learned.
41. Draw a picture showing your favorite part so far in the story.
42. Which illustration did you like best from this part of the story—and why?
43. Make up sentences using at least ten of the vocabulary words.

THE TALE OF MRS. TITTLEMOUSE

Part II

☐ **READ PAGES 230-234 IN <u>The Tale of Mrs. Tittlemouse</u>.**

❧ **FIND OUT WHAT THESE WORDS MEAN:**
1. unnecessarily (p. 230)
2. rose (p. 230)
3. ponderously (p. 230)
4. convinced (p. 230)
5. fast (p. 230)
6. bristles (p. 232)
7. toad (p. 232)
8. distracted (p. 232)
9. scolded (p. 232)
10. objection (p. 232)
11. dreadful (p. 232)
12. smears (p. 232)
13. remains (p. 232)
14. flannel (p. 233)
15. fortnight (p. 233)
16. honey-dew (p. 234)
17. offended (p. 234)

✏ **PLEASE ANSWER THESE IN COMPLETE SENTENCES:**
18. What two things did Mrs. Tittlemouse offer Mr. Jackson to eat?
19. When Mrs. Tittlemouse told Mr. Jackson she had no honey, what did he do?
20. What did Mr. Jackson do to Babbitty Bumble?
21. How did Mr. Jackson help Mrs. Tittlemouse?
22. After Mr. Jackson left, what did Mrs. Tittlemouse do to her door—and why?
23. What did Mrs. Tittlemouse do to her home then (after her sleep)?
24. Who was invited to Mrs. Tittlemouse's home—and what did they do?

✔ **LEARNING MORE:**
25. Draw a picture of your favorite part of this section of the story.
26. Which illustration do you like best from this half of the story? What about it appeals to you?
27. Read this story to a younger child.
28. Make up sentences using at least ten of the vocabulary words.

THE TALE OF JEMIMA PUDDLE-DUCK

Part I

☐ **READ PAGES 159-166a IN <u>The Tale of Jemima Puddle-duck</u>.**

❦ **FIND OUT WHAT THESE WORDS MEAN:**

1. brood (p. 161)
2. annoyed (p. 161)
3. hatch (p. 161)
4. sister-in-law (p. 161)
5. desperate (p. 162)
6. determined (p. 162)
7. right away (p. 162)
8. cart-road (p. 162)
9. poke bonnet (p. 162)
10. flapping (p. 163)
11. skimmed (p. 163)
12. brushwood (p. 163)
13. alighted (p. 163)
14. heavily (p. 163)
15. waddle (p. 163)
16. convenient (p. 163)
17. nesting place (p. 163)
18. fancied (p. 164)
19. fox-gloves (p. 164)
20. startled (p. 164)
21. elegantly (p. 164)
22. prick (p. 164)
23. curiously (p. 164)
24. bushy (p. 164)
25. mighty (p. 164)
26. civil (p. 164)
27. complained (p. 164)
28. superfluous (p. 164)
29. fowl (p. 165)
30. difficulty (p. 165)
31. retired (p. 165)
32. dismal-looking (p. 165)
33. faggots (p. 165)
34. turf (p. 165)
35. by way of (p. 165)
36. residence (p. 165)
37. hospitable (p. 165)
38. tumble-down (p. 165)
39. soap-boxes (p. 165)
40. suffocating (p. 166)
41. vast (p. 166)

✎ **PLEASE ANSWER THESE IN COMPLETE SENTENCES:**

42. What was Jemima Puddle-duck's desire?
43. Where did she decide she'd go search for a nesting place?
44. Describe the gentleman she met in the woods.
45. Referring to page 165, how do you think the fox would teach the hen to mind its own business?
46. What did the gentleman offer Jemima?
47. What should Jemima have been alerted to when she saw the shed filled with feathers?
48. Was the gentleman being honest with Jemima?

✔ **LEARNING MORE:**

49. Learn more about foxes. In the Reading section of your notebook, write about what you have learned.
50. Learn more about ducks. In the Reading section of your notebook, write about what you have learned.
51. What was your favorite illustration for this story so far—and why?
52. Draw a picture of your favorite part of this section of the story.
53. Make up sentences using at least ten of the vocabulary words.

THE TALE OF JEMIMA PUDDLE-DUCK

Part II

❑ **READ PAGES 166b-172 IN The Tale of Jemima Puddle-duck.**

🐛 FIND OUT WHAT THESE WORDS MEAN:

1. polite (p. 166)
2. admired (p. 166)
3. immensely (p. 166)
4. intended (p. 166)
5. sit (p. 166)
6. conscientious (p. 167)
7. provide (p. 167)
8. commence (p. 167)
9. tedious (p. 167)
10. intend (p. 167)
11. dinner-party (p. 167)
12. savoury, (savory)(p. 167)
13. omelette (p. 167)
14. sage (p. 167)
15. thyme (p. 167)
16. lard (p. 167)

17. simpleton (p. 167)
18. suspicious (p. 167)
19. nibbling (p. 167)
20. snippets (p. 167)
21. collie-dog (p. 168)
22. in awe (p. 168)
23. exact (p. 168)
24. position (p. 168)
25. trotted (p. 168)
26. fox-hound (p. 168)
27. butcher (p. 168)
28. burdened (p. 169)
29. opposite (p. 169)
30. glancing (p. 169)
31. uneasily (p. 169)
32. abrupt (p. 169)

33. pattering (p. 170)
34. alarmed (p. 170)
35. awful (p. 170)
36. baying (p. 170)
37. growls (p. 170)
38. howls (p. 170)
39. squealing (p. 170)
40. groans (p. 170)
41. rushed (p. 170)
42. gobbled (p. 170)
43. limping (p. 171)
44. escorted (p. 171)
45. in tears (p. 171)
46. on account of (p. 171)
47. permitted (p. 172)
48. nerves (p. 172)

✏️ PLEASE ANSWER THESE IN COMPLETE SENTENCES:

49. Why was the fox sad to see Jemima go for the evening?
50. What did the fox do with the eggs while Jemima was gone?
51. What did the gentleman ask Jemima to bring back with her the next day?
52. On page 167, the fox almost tells his plans about his real use for the herbs. What word almost slipped out?
53. How did Jemima react to the fox's request to bring the items?
54. In whom did Jemima confide about her plans?
55. Why was the collie described as wise when he listened to Jemima's story?
56. What did the collie immediately do while Jemima went to the woods?
57. What change of character in the gentleman did Jemima notice when she returned?
58. How did this change make her feel?
59. Look at the bottom picture on page 169. Find the three dogs.
60. What did the dogs do for Jemima?
61. What happened to Jemima's eggs?
62. When Jemima laid eggs again, how many hatched?

✔ LEARNING MORE:

63. What lessons can we learn from this story?
64. Draw a picture of your favorite part of the section of the story just read.
65. Which illustration in this part is your favorite—and what do you like best about it?
66. Read this story to a younger child.
67. Make up sentences using at least twelve of the vocabulary words.

THE TALE OF MRS. TIGGY-WINKLE

Part I

☐ **READ PAGES 85-93a IN <u>The Tale of Mrs. Tiggy-winkle</u>.**

🐛 **FIND OUT WHAT THESE WORDS MEAN:**

1. pocket-handkerchiefs (p. 87)
2. pinny (p. 87)
3. paws (p. 87)
4. speckled (p. 87)
5. clucking (p. 87)
6. bright (p. 88)
7. stile (p. 88)
8. scrambled (p. 88)
9. stout (p. 88)
10. pebble (p. 88)
11. spring (p. 89)
12. bubbling (p. 89)
13. egg-cup (p. 89)
14. foot-marks (p. 89)
15. props (p. 89)
16. bracken (p. 89)
17. plaited (p. 89)
18. rushes (p. 89)
19. lily-white (p. 89)
20. frills (p. 89)
21. smooth (p. 89)
22. rusty (p. 89)
23. interrupted (p. 90)
24. flagged (p. 90)
25. beams (p. 90)
26. singey (p. 90)
27. anxiously (p. 90)
28. print (p. 90)
29. gown (p. 90)
30. petticoat (p. 90)
31. sniffle (p. 90)
32. twinkle (p. 90)
33. prickles (p. 90)
34. bob-curtsey (p. 91)
35. excellent (p. 91)
36. clear-starcher (p. 91)
37. scarlet (p. 91)
38. waist-coat (p. 91)
39. clothes-horse (p. 92)
40. damask (p. 92)
41. goffered (p. 93)

✏ **PLEASE ANSWER THESE IN COMPLETE SENTENCES:**

42. What had Lucie lost?
43. What three animals did Lucie talk to about her lost items?
44. What did Lucie believe she saw on the hillside?
45. What did Lucie see at the spring?
46. Describe what (and who) Lucie found in the hillside.

✔ **LEARNING MORE:**

47. Find out more about hedgehogs. In the Reading section of your notebook, write about what you have learned.
48. Name another prickly animal.
49. Which illustration from this section of the story do you like the best? What appeals to you about it?
50. Draw a picture showing your favorite part of the story thus far.
51. Make up sentences using at least twelve of the vocabulary words.

THE TALE OF MRS. TIGGY-WINKLE

Part II

❑ **READ PAGES 93b-100 IN <u>The Tale of Mrs. Tiggy-winkle</u>.**

❧ **FIND OUT WHAT THESE WORDS MEAN:**

1. dipping (p. 95)
2. basin (p. 95)
3. starch (p. 95)
4. dickey (p. 95)
5. particular (p. 95)
6. air (p. 95)
7. fluffy (p. 96)
8. before (p. 97)
9. hair-pins (p. 97)
10. bundles (p. 97)
11. turf (p. 97)
12. door-sill (p. 97)
13. trotted (p. 98)
14. obliged (p. 98)
15. scrambled (p. 99)
16. bill (p. 99)
17. shawl (p. 99)
18. acquainted (p. 100)

✏️ **PLEASE ANSWER THESE IN COMPLETE SENTENCES:**

19. What item was used as a trivet to hold the hot iron?
20. After Mrs. Tiggy-winkle had finished washing and airing the clothes, what did she and Lucie do?
21. Where did Mrs. Tiggy-winkle hide her key?
22. Name four of Mrs. Tiggy-winkle's customers.
23. When Lucie turned to thank Mrs. Tiggy-winkle, what did she find had happened?
24. Do you think it was a dream?

✔ **LEARNING MORE:**

25. Which illustration from this section of the story is your favorite—and why?
26. Draw a picture of your favorite part of the story section read today.
27. Read this story to a younger child.
28. Make up sentences using at least ten of the vocabulary words.

GINGER AND PICKLES

Part I

❑ **READ PAGES 209-216 IN <u>Ginger and Pickles</u>.**

🐝 **FIND OUT WHAT THESE WORDS MEAN:**

1. village (p. 211)
2. convenient (p. 211)
3. spotty (p. 211)
4. farthings (p. 211)
5. snuff (p. 211)
6. boot laces (p. 211)
7. tomcat (p. 211)
8. terrier (p. 211)
9. patronized (p. 212)
10. requested (p. 212)

11. parcels (p. 212)
12. on the contrary (p. 212)
13. gloomily (p. 212)
14. credit (p. 212)
15. unlimited (p. 212)
16. till (p. 213)
17. toffee (p. 213)
18. pennyworth (p. 213)
19. haddock (p. 213)
20. license (p. 215)

21. unpleasant (p. 215)
22. vain (p. 215)
23. intends (p. 215)
24. replied (p. 215)
25. pockets (p. 216)
26. retired (p. 216)
27. accounts (p. 216)
28. sums (p. 216)
29. sealing wax (p. 216)

✏️ **PLEASE ANSWER THESE IN COMPLETE SENTENCES:**

30. Who was Ginger? Pickles?
31. Name three customers of the Ginger & Pickles shop.
32. Why did Ginger ask Pickles to wait on the mice?
33. What was the difference between Ginger & Pickles' store and that of Tabitha Twitchit?
34. What other story by the same author had Tabitha Twitchit in it?
35. What problem did Ginger and Pickles have?
36. Describe how people use credit. What problems do you think there might be about not paying cash right away?
37. For what did Ginger and Pickles need the money?

✔ **LEARNING MORE:**

38. Learn more about dogs. In the Reading section of your notebook, write about what you have learned.
39. Which illustration from this section was your favorite—and why?
40. Draw a picture of your favorite part of the story so far.
41. Make up sentences using at least ten of the vocabulary words.

GINGER AND PICKLES

Part II

☐ **READ PAGES 217-222 IN <u>Ginger and Pickles</u>.**

❦ **FIND OUT WHAT THESE WORDS MEAN:**

1. fit (p. 217)
2. rushes (p. 217)
3. spluttered (p. 217)
4. treacle (p. 217)
5. hoarse (p. 217)
6. notice (p. 217)
7. bead (p. 217)
8. length (p. 218)
9. summons (p. 218)
10. rates (p. 218)

11. shutters (p. 218)
12. removed (p. 218)
13. warren (p. 219)
14. occupation (p. 219)
15. pursues (p. 219)
16. stout (p. 219)
17. gamekeeper (p. 219)
18. inconvenience (p. 219)
19. tradesmen's (p. 220)
20. seed-wig (p. 220)

21. retail (p. 221)
22. poster (p. 221)
23. co-operative (p. 221)
24. 'ticing (enticing) (p. 221)
25. crammed (p. 222)
26. canisters (p. 222)
27. flustered (p. 222)
28. remarkable (p. 222)
29. assortment (p. 222)
30. bargains (p. 222)

✐ **PLEASE ANSWER THESE IN COMPLETE SENTENCES:**

31. What message did the policeman doll leave in the store?
32. What was the solution that Ginger and Pickles decided upon for their problem?
33. What did the dog and cat do after they made that decision?
34. What happened at Tabitha Twitchit's shop then?
35. What did Mr. John Dormouse and his daughter begin to sell?
36. What was the quality of their products?
37. Who reopened the store?
38. What was her policy about payments?

✔ **LEARNING MORE:**

39. Read Romans 13:8a in The Holy Bible to find out what God thinks of credit.
40. Which illustration from this section was your favorite—and why?
41. Draw a poster for Sally Henny Penny's new store.
42. Read this story to a younger child.
43. Make up sentences using at least twelve of the vocabulary words.

THE TALE OF JOHNNY TOWN-MOUSE

Part I

❏ **READ PAGES 317-324 IN <u>The Tale of Johnny Town-Mouse</u>.**

❧ **FIND OUT WHAT THESE WORDS MEAN:**

1. hamper (p. 319)
2. carrier (p. 319)
3. wicker (p. 319)
4. fright (p. 320)
5. cart (p. 320)
6. jolting (p. 320)
7. clattering (p. 320)
8. trembled (p. 320)
9. jumbled (p. 320)
10. sixpence (p. 320)
11. banged (p. 320)
12. rumbled (p. 320)
13. canary (p. 320)
14. steam engine (p. 320)
15. sprang (p. 321)
16. exclaiming (p. 321)
17. poker (p. 321)
18. skirting board (p. 321)
19. exclamation (p. 322)
20. instantly (p. 322)
21. recovered (p. 322)
22. utmost (p. 322)
23. tails (p. 322)
24. insignificant (p. 322)
25. well bred (p. 322)
26. personal (p. 322)
27. remarks (p. 322)
28. courses (p. 322)
29. elegant (p. 322)
30. anxious (p. 322)
31. company (p. 322)
32. continual (p. 323)
33. skirmishing (p. 323)
34. failed (p. 323)
35. faint (p. 323)
36. honestly (p. 323)
37. exclusively (p. 323)
38. visitors (p. 323)
39. preferred (p. 323)
40. miserable (p. 323)
41. fender (p. 323)
42. accustomed (p. 324)
43. reared (p. 324)
44. roots (p. 324)
45. racketted (p. 324)
46. smears (p. 324)
47. longed (p. 324)
48. peaceful (p. 324)
49. bank (p. 324)
50. disagreed (p. 324)
51. prevented (p. 324)
52. inquired (p. 324)
53. dull (p. 324)

✎ **PLEASE ANSWER THESE IN COMPLETE SENTENCES:**

54. What did Timmy Willie climb into and then fall fast asleep?
55. Where was Timmy Willie taken?
56. Did Timmy Willie know where he was taken? How did he feel?
57. After he escaped from the hamper, where did Timmy Willie go?
58. When Timmy saw the town mice elegantly dressed, he compared and felt embarrassed about how he looked. Read Matthew 6:28-29 and Exodus 20:17 in The Holy Bible. What does it say?
59. How did Timmy feel about the noises from upstairs?
60. Compare the food Timmy was used to with that of Johnny Town-Mouse. What did each eat and where did each get his food?
61. What were the two things that Timmy Willie missed?

✔ **LEARNING MORE:**

62. Learn more about wicker. In the Reading section of your notebook, write about what you have learned.
63. Which illustration from this part of the story was your favorite—and why?
64. Draw a picture of your favorite part of the story so far.
65. Make up sentences using at least twelve of the vocabulary words.

THE TALE OF JOHNNY TOWN-MOUSE

Part II

☐ **READ PAGES 325-330 IN <u>The Tale of Johnny Town-Mouse</u>.**

❧ FIND OUT WHAT THESE WORDS MEAN:

1. burrow (p. 325)
2. shell (p. 325)
3. store (p. 325)
4. peep (p. 325)
5. throstles (p. 325)
6. pinks (p. 325)
7. refuge (p. 325)
8. coal-cellar (p. 325)
9. resumed (p. 325)
10. confess (p. 325)

11. endeavoured (p. 325) (endeavored)
12. entertain (p. 325)
13. digestion (p. 326)
14. huffily (p. 326)
15. withered (p. 326)
16. half promised (p. 327)
17. spick and span (p. 327)
18. open arms (p. 327)
19. harmless (p. 328)

20. middling (p. 328)
21. paying (p. 328)
22. seaside (p. 328)
23. board (p. 328)
24. particular (p. 328)
25. racket (p. 329)
26. clippings (p. 329)
27. settle (p. 329)
28. suits (p. 330)
29. prefer (p. 330)

✎ **PLEASE ANSWER THESE IN COMPLETE SENTENCES:**

30. How did Timmy Willie explain his rainy (and sunny) days?

31. How did Johnny act towards Timmy Willie when Timmy said he missed the country?

32. What day of the week did Timmy Willie take his journey back to the garden?

33. How did Johnny Town-Mouse like the country? Where did he decide to live?

34. Where did the author, Beatrix Potter, prefer to live?

✔ **LEARNING MORE:**

35. In which do you and your family live—the city, a small town, or the country? Explain at least one reason you like where you live.

36. Which illustration from this part of the story is your favorite—and why?

37. Draw a picture of your favorite part of this section of the story.

38. Read this story to a younger child.

39. Make up sentences using at least ten of the vocabulary words.

THE TALE OF TIMMY TIPTOES

Part I

☐ **READ PAGES 235-243a IN <u>The Tale of Timmy Tiptoes</u>.**

🍎 **FIND OUT WHAT THESE WORDS MEAN:**

1. thatched (p. 237)	11. money-box (p. 239)	21. confesses (p. 241)
2. whisked (p. 237)	12. commotion (p. 239)	22. peck (p. 242)
3. chuckled (p. 237)	13. flock (p. 240)	23. stunned (p. 242)
4. prudent (p. 237)	14. rushed (p. 241)	24. ventured (p. 242)
5. thicket (p. 238)	15. innocent (p. 241)	25. senses (p. 243)
6. twig (p. 238)	16. mischief (p. 241)	26. groaned (p. 243)
7. hollow (p. 238)	17. fright (p. 241)	27. chirpy (p. 243)
8. stumps (p. 238)	18. figure (p. 241)	28. striped (p. 243)
9. woodpecker (p. 239)	19. dreadfully (p. 241)	29. nightcap (p. 243)
10. rattled (p. 239)	20. a wonder (p. 241)	30. provisions (p. 243)

✏️ **PLEASE ANSWER THESE IN COMPLETE SENTENCES:**

31. What type of squirrel was Timmy Tiptoes?
32. Where was the nest of Timmy and Goody Tiptoes located?
33. What did Timmy tell Goody they needed to go get—and why?
34. Where did Timmy and Goody work, gathering nuts?
35. Where did Timmy and Goody store their nuts?
36. What problem did many squirrels have with their nuts?
37. What was the name of the most forgetful squirrel?
38. What were the two bird songs that were misunderstood by the squirrels and which caused the trouble for Timmy and Goody?
39. What did the group of squirrels do to Timmy?
40. How did Timmy and Goody each feel about Timmy being gone?
41. What did Chippy Hackee do for Timmy?

✔ **LEARNING MORE:**

42. Which illustration from this part is your favorite—and why?
43. Draw a picture of your favorite part of this section of the story.
44. Learn more about chipmunks. In the Reading section of your notebook, write about what you have learned.
45. Make up sentences using at least twelve of the vocabulary words.

THE TALE OF TIMMY TIPTOES

Part II

❑ **READ PAGES 243b-250 IN <u>The Tale of Timmy Tiptoes</u>.**

🍂 **FIND OUT WHAT THESE WORDS MEAN:**
1. confined (p. 243)
2. doubted (p. 244)
3. fell out (p. 245)
4. fie (p. 246)
5. padlock (p. 249)

✏️ **PLEASE ANSWER THESE IN COMPLETE SENTENCES:**
6. What did Goody Tiptoes learn from Mrs. Chippy Hackee?
7. What was Timmy's problem in the hollow tree?
8. What did Timmy do when he heard Goody's voice at the tree hole?
9. How did Timmy finally get out of the tree?
10. How much longer did Chippy Hackee stay away from his home?
11. What finally persuaded Chippy Hackee to return home?
12. From the illustration on page 2 49, how many squirrel babies did Timmy and Goody Tiptoes have?
13. Why is Mrs. Chippy Hackee shaking her umbrella at a bird in the illustration on page 250?

✔ **LEARNING MORE:**
14. Looking at the illustrations, how do squirrels and chipmunks differ in appearance?
15. Which illustration from this part of the story is your favorite—and why?
16. Draw a picture of your favorite part of this section of the story.
17. Read this story to a younger child.
18. Make up sentences using at least three of the vocabulary words.

THE PIE AND THE PATTY-PAN

Part I

☐ **READ PAGES 101-107 IN <u>The Pie and the Patty-pan</u>.**

❦ **FIND OUT WHAT THESE WORDS MEAN:**

1. rim (p. 103)
2. punctually (p. 103)
3. veal (p. 103)
4. patty-pan (p. 105)
5. steam (p. 105)
6. considered (p. 105)
7. delighted (p. 105)
8. cleverness (p. 105)
9. meantime (p. 105)
10. ornamental (p. 105)
11. intended (p. 105)
12. stiff (p. 105)
13. delicate (p. 105)
14. tender (p. 105)
15. minced (p. 105)
16. genteel (p. 106)
17. infinitely (p. 106)
18. superior (p. 106)
19. hearth (p. 106)
20. mantelpiece (p. 106)
21. jug (p. 107)
22. peeped (p. 107)
23. comfortable (p. 107)
24. packet (p. 107)
25. lump (p. 107)
26. bowed (p. 107)

✐ **PLEASE ANSWER THESE IN COMPLETE SENTENCES:**

27. Who were the two main characters in the story—and what kind of animals were they?
28. What did Ribby write to Duchess?
29. What troubled Duchess about this invitation?
30. What did Duchess do to "solve" her problem?
31. Which oven did Ribby use for her pie?
32. What errands were Duchess and Ribby each doing before the party?

✔ **LEARNING MORE:**

33. Which illustration from this part of the story is your favorite—and why?
34. Draw a picture of your favorite part of this section of the story.
35. Make up sentences using at least ten of the vocabulary words.

THE PIE AND THE PATTY-PAN

Part II

❑ **READ PAGES 108-113a IN <u>The Pie and the Patty-pan</u>.**

❧ **FIND OUT WHAT THESE WORDS MEAN:**

1. required (p. 108)
2. pleasant (p. 108)
3. gossip (p. 108)
4. disdainful (p. 108)
5. afterwards (p. 108)
6. conversation (p. 108)
7. odd (p. 109)
8. shams (p. 109)
9. coat (p. 109)
10. assured (p. 109)
11. larder (p. 109)
12. lilac (p. 110)
13. silk (p. 110)
14. gown (p. 110)
15. embroidered (p. 110)
16. muslin (p. 110)
17. tippet (p. 110)
18. hob (p. 110)
19. shade (p. 111)
20. marmalade (p. 112)
21. toothsome (p. 113)
22. quicker (p. 113)

✎ **PLEASE ANSWER THESE IN COMPLETE SENTENCES:**

23. Mrs. Tabitha Twitchit spoke badly against Duchess. Why do you think she might have done this?
24. Where did Ribby get muffins?
25. The animals in the book did not carry their items in paper bags. What did they use?
26. What puzzled Duchess after she put her pie into the top oven?
27. What did each of the animals do to prepare themselves for the supper?
28. What hostess gift did Duchess bring to Ribby?
29. What did Duchess begin to say to Ribby about the smell of the pie?
30. What did Duchess miss seeing while she was under the table?
31. What was Duchess concerned that Ribby would put into the pie?

✔ **LEARNING MORE:**

32. Learn more about baskets and basket-making. In the Reading section of your notebook, write about what you have learned.
33. Which illustration from this part of the story is your favorite—and why?
34. Draw a picture of your favorite part of this section of the story.
35. Make up sentences using at least ten of the vocabulary words.

THE PIE AND THE PATTY-PAN

Part III

❑ **READ PAGES 113b-118 IN <u>The Pie and the Patty-pan</u>.**

🐛 **FIND OUT WHAT THESE WORDS MEAN:**

1. perplexed (p. 113)
2. disapprove (p. 113)
3. undesirable (p. 114)
4. lower (p. 114)
5. scoop (p. 114)
6. aghast (p. 114)
7. tilted (p. 114)
8. moaned (p. 114)
9. whined (p. 114)
10. prop (p. 114)
11. scalloped (p. 114)

12. smithy (p. 115)
13. occupied (p. 115)
14. rusty (p. 115)
15. gammon (p. 115)
16. accompanied (p. 115)
17. alacrity (p. 115)
18. conspicuous (p. 115)
19. mournfully (p. 116)
20. grate (p. 116)
21. crackled (p. 116)
22. started (p. 116)

23. reflected (p. 116)
24. awkward (p. 116)
25. pulse (p. 116)
26. magpie (p. 116)
27. sidled (p. 116)
28. triumphantly (p. 117)
29. admirable (p. 117)
30. affectionately (p. 117)
31. jackdaws (p. 117)

✎ **PLEASE ANSWER THESE IN COMPLETE SENTENCES:**

32. How many muffins did Ribby have? How many helpings of pie for Duchess?
33. What did Duchess try to convince Ribby?
34. For what two reasons did Ribby not use a patty-pan?
35. What did Duchess think she had done?
36. What did Ribby do for Duchess?
37. Why did Duchess say Dr. Maggotty was a pie?
38. Who peeped out of her store and saw Ribby and Dr. Maggotty running down the road?
39. While Ribby was gone, what did Duchess realize about the patty-pan?
40. After Duchess found her own pie still in the oven, what was her plan to keep it a secret?
41. What did Duchess see when she secretly returned to Ribby's yard?
42. How did Ribby feel when she saw the pie-dish and the patty-pan lying in the backyard?

✔ **LEARN MORE**

43. There is a saying: "What a tangled web we weave, when first we practice to deceive."
    How did Ribby's first lie get her into more and more trouble?
44. Learn more about magpies and crows. In the Reading section of your notebook, write
    about what you have learned.
45. Which illustration from this part of the story is your favorite—and why?
46. Draw a picture of your favorite part of this section of the story.
47. Read this story to a younger child.
48. Make up sentences using at least twelve of the vocabulary words.

THE ROLY-POLY PUDDING

Part I

☐ **READ PAGES 173-181 IN <u>The Roly-Poly Pudding</u>.**

🐛 **FIND OUT WHAT THESE WORDS MEAN:**

1. anxious (p. 175)
2. continually (p. 175)
3. mewing (p. 175)
4. spare (p. 175)
5. dust (p. 175)
6. attics (p. 175)
7. queer (p. 175)
8. jagged (p. 175)
9. wainscot (p. 175)
10. distracted (p. 175)
11. dreadfully (p. 175)
12. barrel (p. 177)
13. shedding (p. 177)
14. cat's cradle (p. 177)
15. unruly (p. 178)
16. whip (p. 178)
17. soot (p. 178)
18. fender (p. 178)
19. thoroughly (p. 179)
20. rummaged (p. 179)
21. tearfully (p. 179)
22. roly-poly (p. 180)
23. distinctly (p. 181)

✏️ **PLEASE ANSWER THESE IN COMPLETE SENTENCES:**

24. What were Mrs. Tabitha Twitchit's three children named?
25. Were they obedient kittens?
26. Mrs. Twitchit began looking for Tom. What conclusion did she come to about her son, Tom?
27. While their mom was looking for Tom, what did Mittens and Moppet each do?
28. Who came to the door—and why?
29. What was Ribby's opinion of Tom?
30. What did Ribby volunteer to do?
31. What did Ribby and Tabitha hear under the attic floor?
32. What had Moppet seen while she was hidden?
33. What had Mittens seen while she was hidden?

✔ **LEARNING MORE:**

34. Which illustration from this part of the story is your favorite—and why?
35. Draw a picture of your favorite part of this section of the story.
36. Make up sentences using at least ten of the vocabulary words.

THE ROLY-POLY PUDDING

Part II

☐ **READ PAGES 182-188 IN <u>The Roly-Poly Pudding</u>.**

❦ **FIND OUT WHAT THESE WORDS MEAN:**

1. convenient (p. 182)
2. choky (p. 182)
3. balancing (p. 182)
4. slates (p. 184)
5. singe (p. 184)
6. stack (p. 184)
7. sweep (p. 185)
8. confusing (p. 185)
9. flue (p. 185)
10. mutton (p. 185)
11. gnawing (p. 185)
12. scarcely (p. 186)
13. skirting board (p. 186)
14. heap (p. 186)
15. stuffy (p. 186)
16. fusty (p. 186)
17. lath (p. 186)
18. plaster (p. 186)
19. opposite (p. 186)
20. smuts (p. 187)
21. chattering (p. 187)
22. pattering (p. 187)
23. bundle (p. 187)
24. snuff (p. 187)
25. dumpling (p. 187)
26. considering (p. 187)
27. breadcrumbs (p. 188)

✎ **PLEASE ANSWER THESE IN COMPLETE SENTENCES:**

28. Who did Ribby suggest they call for help?

29. Meanwhile, where had Tom crawled in exploring?

30. What did he smell?

31. When he fell down the hole, where did he land?

32. What two creatures did he meet—and what were their names?

33. What did the two rats do to Tom Kitten?

34. What did Samuel Whiskers want his wife to make for him?

✔ **LEARNING MORE:**

35. Learn more about rats. In the Reading section of your notebook, write about what you have learned.

36. Which illustration from this part of the story is your favorite—and why?

37. Draw a picture of your favorite part of this section of the story.

38. Make up sentences using at least twelve of the vocabulary words.

The Roly-Poly Pudding

Part III

☐ **READ PAGES 189-196 IN <u>The Roly-Poly Pudding</u>.**

❦ **FIND OUT WHAT THESE WORDS MEAN:**

1. observe (p. 189)
2. critically (p. 189)
3. judge (p. 189)
4. unfortunate (p. 189)
5. assist (p. 189)
6. squirmed (p. 189)
7. spat (p. 190)
8. rasping (p. 191)
9. yelping (p. 191)
10. attentively (p. 191)
11. discovered (p. 191)
12. interrupted (p. 191)
13. property (p. 191)
14. depart (p. 191)
15. obliged (p. 191)
16. persuaded (p. 191)
17. proved (p. 191)
18. indigestible (p. 191)
19. urge (p. 191)
20. contrary (p. 191)
21. counterpane (p. 191)
22. gimlet (p. 191)
23. recovered (p. 192)
24. peeled (p. 192)
25. separately (p. 192)
26. currants (p. 192)
27. wheelbarrow (p. 192)
28. post (p. 192)
29. shrill (p. 193)
30. tones (p. 193)
31. leave (p. 193)
32. hauled (p. 193)
33. haymow (p. 193)
34. distracted (p. 194)
35. oats (p. 194)
36. bran (p. 194)
37. meal (p. 194)
38. descended (p. 194)
39. plenty (p. 195)
40. employment (p. 195)
41. charge (p. 195)
42. dozen (p. 195)

✐ **PLEASE ANSWER THESE IN COMPLETE SENTENCES:**

43. What did Samuel and Anna Maria each go to get?
44. Who saw Tom tied up and mewing—and what did he do to help?
45. After the two rats returned, what did they do to Tom?
46. What did the rats hear and what decision did they make?
48. Who rescued Tom Kitten?
49. What did the cat family do with the dumpling?
50. What was John making—and for whom?
51. Who and what did the author see as she went to the post office that afternoon?
52. What color dress was Miss Potter wearing?
53. Where did Samuel and Anna Maria Whiskers settle?
54. What new problem did Farmer Potatoes have?
55. What did Moppet and Mittens become good at doing?
56. How did Tom Kitten feel about rats?

✔ **LEARNING MORE:**

57. There is a saying: "Curiosity kills the cat." How did Tom Kitten's curiosity get him into trouble?
58. Which illustration from this section is your favorite—and why?
59. Draw a picture of your favorite part of this section of the story.
60. Read this story to a younger child.
61. Make up sentences using at least twelve of the vocabulary words.

THE TAILOR OF GLOUCESTER

Part I

❑ **READ PAGES 37-42 IN <u>The Tailor of Gloucester</u>.**

🍎 **FIND OUT WHAT THESE WORDS MEAN:**

1. swords (p. 39)	12. satin (p. 39)	23. nought (p. 39)	34. sufficient (p. 40)
2. periwigs (p. 39)	13. pompadour (p. 39)	24. bitter (p. 39)	35. trap-doors (p. 41)
3. full-skirted (p. 39)	14. lutestring (p. 39)	25. corded (p. 39)	36. shuffled (p. 41)
4. lappets (p. 39)	15. expensive (p. 39)	26. pansies (p. 39)	37. fortune (p. 41)
5. ruffles (p. 39)	16. spectacles (p. 39)	27. cream (p. 39)	38. ravelling (p. 41)
6. waistcoats (p. 39)	17. pinched (p. 39)	28. gauze (p. 39)	39. groat (p. 41)
7. paduasoy (p. 39)	18. thread-bare (p. 39)	29. worsted (p. 39)	40. pipkin (p. 41)
8. taffeta (p. 39)	19. waste (p. 39)	30. chenille (p. 39)	41. twist (p. 42)
9. tailor (p. 39)	20. embroidere d(p. 39)	31. shears (p. 40)	42. bias (p. 42)
10. cross-legged (p. 39)	21. snippets (p. 39)	32. mobs (p. 40)	43. sufficeth (p. 42)
11. snippeted (p. 39)	22. breadths (p. 39)	33. leaded (p. 40)	44. crockery (p. 42)

✏️ **PLEASE ANSWER THESE IN COMPLETE SENTENCES:**

45. Did the tailor have lots of money?
46. Describe what the tailor looked like and how he worked.
47. Was the tailor wasteful with his fabrics?
48. What did the tailor say the scraps of material were good for?
49. What was the project the tailor was working on around Christmas time?
50. When the tailor left for home after his day's work, what was the condition of the project and the tailor's shop?
51. What was missing to complete the project?
52. Describe how the tailor lived.
53. What was the name of the tailor's cat?
54. What did the cat do with the mice he caught?
55. What were the four things the tailor asked the cat to get from the market?
56. While the tailor was sitting by the fire, what did he begin to hear?

✔ **LEARNING MORE:**

57. Find Gloucester on a map of England.
58. Feel (with clean hands!) different kinds of fabrics. Which kinds do you like best?
59. Which illustration from this part is your favorite—and why?
60. Draw a picture of your favorite part of this section of the story.
61. Make up sentences using at least twelve of the vocabulary words.

THE TAILOR OF GLOUCESTER

Part II

❑ **READ PAGES 43-47a IN <u>The Tailor of Gloucester</u>.**

🐭 **FIND OUT WHAT THESE WORDS MEAN:**

1. curtsey (p. 43)
2. mumbling (p. 43)
3. tambour (p. 43)
4. floss (p. 43)
5. extraordinary (p. 43)
6. chorus (p. 44)
7. watch-beetle (p. 44)

8. basins (p. 44)
9. vexed (p. 44)
10. fever (p. 45)
11. four-post (p. 45)
12. barred (p. 46)
13. hinder (p. 46)
14. trudging (p. 46)

15. beasts (p. 47)
16. cathedral (p. 47)
17. echo (p. 47)
18. chimes (p. 47)
19. gables (p. 47)

✏️ **PLEASE ANSWER THESE IN COMPLETE SENTENCES:**

20. What did the tailor discover underneath the pieces of china?
21. How many buttonholes did the tailor need to make?
22. What day was it when he sat by the fire?
23. What day did he need to have the coat done?
24. Who was listening as the tailor spoke to himself?
25. When Simpkin returned from the errand, what kind of a mood was he in—and why?
26. What did Simpkin want when he got home?
27. What did the cat do with the package of thread?
28. How did Simpkin act that evening?
29. How was the tailor feeling—and for how long?
30. How did the mice enter the shop, even though the door was locked?

✔ **LEARNING MORE:**

31. Learn more about sewing. Watch your mom (or a seamstress or tailor) sew. In the Reading section of your notebook, write about what you have learned.
32. Which illustration from this part of the story is your favorite—and why?
33. Draw a picture of your favorite part of this section of the story.
34. Make up sentences using at least seven of the vocabulary words.

THE TAILOR OF GLOUCESTER

Part III

☐ **READ PAGES 47b-52 IN <u>The Tailor of Gloucester</u>.**

❧ **FIND OUT WHAT THESE WORDS MEAN:**

1. cocks (p. 47)
2. garret (p. 47)
3. eaves (p. 47)
4. starlings (p. 47)
5. twittering (p. 47)
6. provoking ((p. 47)
7. lattice (p. 47)
8. bats (p. 48)
9. frost (p. 48)
10. mysterious (p. 48)
11. kyloe (p. 48)
12. sieve (p. 48)
13. grind (p. 48)
14. thimbles (p. 49)
15. mark (p. 49)
16. nicks (p. 50)
17. repentant (p. 50)
18. facings (p. 51)
19. poppies (p. 51)
20. corn-flowers (p. 51)
21. wanting (p. 51)

✏ **PLEASE ANSWER THESE IN COMPLETE SENTENCES:**

22. What did Simpkin see when he peeped into the tailor shop on Christmas eve?
23. What did the mice all shout together to Simpkin?
24. How did Simpkin feel after he returned home?
25. What did he do about that feeling?
26. What day did the tailor wake up and feel better?
27. When the tailor and the cat went to the shop on Christmas morning, what did they find?
28. How do you think the tailor felt when he saw the coat on the table?
29. What message did the mice leave pinned onto the waistcoat?
30. How did the tailor profit from completing (with help) this project?

✔ **LEARNING MORE:**

31. Learn more about some of the different kinds of flowers mentioned in this story. In the Reading section of your notebook, write about what you have learned.
32. Learn more about embroidery. In the Reading section of your notebook, write about what you have learned.
33. Which illustration from this part of the story is your favorite—and why?
34. Draw a picture of your favorite part of this section of the story.
35. Read this story to a younger child.
36. Make up sentences using at least ten of the vocabulary words.

THE TALE OF PIGLING BLAND

Part I

❑ **READ PAGES 281-291 IN <u>The Tale of Pigling Bland</u>.**

🐿 **FIND OUT WHAT THESE WORDS MEAN:**

1. appetites (p. 283)
2. pride (p. 283)
3. hoops (p. 283)
4. trough (p. 283)
5. disgrace (p. 283)
6. grunted (p. 283)
7. rooting (p. 284)
8. worthy (p. 284)
9. brought up (p. 284)
10. addressed (p. 286)
11. hind (p. 287)
12. sedate (p. 287)
13. solemnly (p. 287)
14. trickled (p. 287)
15. observe (p. 287)
16. milestones (p. 287)
17. gobble (p. 287)

18. herring (p. 287)
19. impressively (p. 287)
20. boundary (p. 287)
21. attending (p. 287)
22. gravely (p. 287)
23. volatile (p. 287)
24. bundle (p. 288)
25. conversation (p. 288)
26. appropriate (p. 288)
27. moral (p. 288)
28. sentiments (p. 288)
29. screws (p. 288)
30. preserve (p. 289)
31. emergencies (p. 289)
32. doubtfully (p. 289)
33. reproved (p. 289)
34. scrumply (p. 289)

35. visibly (p. 289)
36. conclude (p. 290)
37. sauntered (p. 290)
38. damp (p. 290)
39. subdued (p. 290)
40. disposed (p. 290)
41. dejectedly (p. 290)
42. shocked (p. 290)
43. hiring (p. 290)
44. deplorable (p. 290)
45. frivolity (p. 290)
46. glanced (p. 291)
47. wistfully (p. 291)
48. obediently (p. 291)
49. disagreeable (p. 291)

✏️ **PLEASE ANSWER THESE IN COMPLETE SENTENCES:**

50. How many piglings did Aunt Pettitoes have?
51. Name two of the pigs.
52. What were two problems with the pigs?
53. What was Aunt Pettitoe's solution to the problem of the pigs?
54. What did Pigling Bland and Alexander need to take with them?
55. What happened to Alexander on the way to market?
56. Pigling Bland did not want to go to market. What did he really wish he could do?

✔ **LEARNING MORE:**

57. Learn more about pigs. In the Reading section of your notebook, write about what you have learned.
58. Which illustration from this part of the story is your favorite—and why?
59. Draw a picture of your favorite part of this section of the story.
60. Make up sentences using at least twelve of the vocabulary words.

THE TALE OF PIGLING BLAND

Part II

❑ **READ PAGES 292-298 IN <u>The Tale of Pigling Bland</u>.**

🍎 FIND OUT WHAT THESE WORDS MEAN:

1. hut (p. 292)
2. disturbed (p. 293)
3. cockerel (p. 293)
4. broody (p. 293)
5. roosting (p. 293)
6. determined (p. 293)
7. lantern (p. 293)
8. fowls (p. 293)
9. scruff (p. 294)
10. cackling (p. 294)
11. jerks (p. 294)
12. contrived (p. 294)
13. offensively (p. 294)

14. elderly (p. 294)
15. coppy (p. 294)
16. shyly (p. 294)
17. smothered (p. 294)
18. eyed (p. 294)
19. flung (p. 295)
20. porridge (p. 295)
21. suppressed (p. 295)
22. discreetly (p. 295)
23. consulted (p. 296)
24. almanac (p. 296)
25. grudged (p. 296)
26. flitch (p. 296)

27. undecidedly (p. 296)
28. enjoining (p. 296)
29. meddle (p. 296)
30. nought (p. 296)
31. distrusted (p. 296)
32. leisure (p. 296)
33. cottage (p. 296)
34. peelings (p. 296)
35. pause (p. 298)
36. tip-toe (p. 298)
37. affable (p. 298)
38. account (p. 298)

✏️ PLEASE ANSWER THESE IN COMPLETE SENTENCES:

39. Did Pigling Bland ever make it to the market?
40. Where did he sleep that night?
41. What happened to him in the morning?
42. While Mr. Piperson was gone, what did Pigling Bland do?
43. What did Pigling Bland wear?
44. While Pigling was eating his supper, what surprised him?

✔ LEARNING MORE:

45. Learn more about hens. In the Reading section of your notebook, write about what you have learned.
46. Which illustration from this part is your favorite—and why?
47. Draw a picture of your favorite part of this section of the story.
48. Make up sentences using at least twelve of the vocabulary words.

THE TALE OF PIGLING BLAND

Part III

❏ **READ PAGES 299-308 IN <u>The Tale of Pigling Bland</u>.**

❦ **FIND OUT WHAT THESE WORDS MEAN:**

1. twinkly (p. 299)
2. screwed up (p. 299)
3. double (p. 299)
4. turned up (p. 299)
5. hastily (p. 299)
6. fled (p. 299)
7. scruple (p. 299)
8. horrified (p. 299)
9. gratitude (p. 300)
10. embarrassing (p. 300)
11. obliged (p. 301)
12. pretend (p. 301)
13. firelight (p. 301)
14. alarmed (p. 301)
15. dismayed (p. 301)

16. successfully (p. 301)
17. peaky (p. 302)
18. antimacassar (p. 302)
19. chirping (p. 302)
20. crickets (p. 302)
21. snores (p. 302)
22. overhead (p. 302)
23. peaceable (p. 302)
24. untidy (p. 303)
25. crossing (p. 304)
26. moor (p. 304)
27. dazzle (p. 304)
28. crept (p. 304)
29. valleys (p. 304)
30. nestled (p. 304)

31. orchards (p. 304)
32. commenced (p. 304)
33. stirring (p. 305)
34. crossly (p. 305)
35. ploughing, plowing (p. 305)
36. reins (p. 305)
37. flapped (p. 305)
38. grocer (p. 305)
39. frightfully (p. 306)
40. lame (p. 306)
41. intent (p. 306)
42. shied (p. 306)
43. snorted (p. 306)
44. crossways (p. 306)
45. vacantly (p. 306)

46. deaf (p. 306)
47. fumbled (p. 306)
48. dissatisfied (p. 306)
49. asthmatically (p. 306)
50. advertisement (p. 306)
51. column (p. 306)
52. reward (p. 306)
53. trap (p. 306)
54. stock-still (p. 307)
55. pelted (p. 308)
56. petticoats (p. 308)
57. fluttered (p. 308)
58. cut (p. 308)
59. turf (p. 308)
60. rushes (p. 308)

✎ **PLEASE ANSWER THESE IN COMPLETE SENTENCES:**

61. How did Pig-wig get to be at Mr. Piperson's?
62. What did Pigling Bland do for Pig-wig after she fell asleep?
63. What did Pigling do that evening?
64. When did the two pigs leave Mr. Piperson's house?
65. What did Pigling Bland begin to do when he saw a tradesman's cart and what did he tell Pig-wig?
66. Name two things Pigling Bland pretended to be while they were talking with the man in the cart.
67. After the man began to drive away, why did Pigling Bland tell Pig-wig not to go yet?
68. Do you think Pigling was going to get to have his wish?

✔ **LEARNING MORE:**

69. Which illustration from this part of the story is your favorite—and why?
70. Draw a picture of your favorite part of this section of the story.
71. Read this story to a younger child.
72. Make up sentences using at least twelve of the vocabulary words.

THE TALE OF MR. TOD

Part I

☐ **READ PAGES 251-259a IN <u>The Tale of Mr. Tod</u>.**

🐛 **FIND OUT WHAT THESE WORDS MEAN:**

1. well-behaved (p. 253)
2. disagreeable (p. 253)
3. bear (p. 253)
4. habit (p. 253)
5. stick-house (p. 253)
6. coppice (p. 253)
7. causing (p. 253)
8. terror (p. 253)
9. pollard (p. 253)
10. generally (p. 253)
11. crag (p. 253)
12. seldom (p. 253)
13. scarce (p. 254)
14. wicked (p. 254)

15. otters (p. 254)
16. painful (p. 254)
17. stricken (p. 254)
18. burrow (p. 254)
19. conversed (p. 254)
20. cordially (p. 254)
21. spud (p. 254)
22. scarcity (p. 254)
23. accused (p. 254)
24. poaching (p. 254)
25. pig-nuts (p. 255)
26. vegetarian (p. 255)
27. confess (p. 256)
28. undeniable (p. 256)

29. wood sorrel (p. 257)
30. darnel (p. 257)
31. thicket (p. 257)
32. hyacinths (p. 257)
33. proof (p. 257)
34. bolted (p. 257)
35. briar (p. 257)
36. displayed (p. 259)
37. lamentable (p. 259)
38. discretion (p. 259)
39. reflectively (p. 259)
40. hopeful (p. 259)
41. circumstances (p. 259)
42. compose (p. 259)

✏️ **PLEASE ANSWER THESE IN COMPLETE SENTENCES:**

43. Who were the two disagreeable creatures in the story and what kind of animals were they?
44. Describe each of them.
45. What happened one day with Mr. Bouncer Bunny, his grandchildren, and Mr. Tommy Brock?
46. Was it wise for Mr. Bunny to do what he did?
47. Did he admit what had happened to Flopsy and Benjamin? Is that right?
48. How did Flopsy and Benjamin each react to coming home and finding their babies gone? (How did they feel and what did they do?)
49. What had Tommy Brock taken the bunnies in?
50. When Benjamin came to Mr. Tod's house, how did they know the fox was home?
51. Who did Benjamin meet after that and what was he doing?
52. How many bunnies had Mr. Brock taken?
53. What hopeful news did Peter have for Benjamin and the rabbit babies?

✔ **LEARNING MORE:**

54. Learn more about badgers. In the Reading section of your notebook, write about what you have learned.
55. Which illustration from this part of the story is your favorite—and why?
56. Draw a picture of your favorite part of this section of the story.
57. Make up sentences using at least twelve of the vocabulary words.

THE TALE OF MR. TOD

Part II

☐ **READ PAGES 259b-266a IN <u>The Tale of Mr. Tod</u>.**

🐛 **FIND OUT WHAT THESE WORDS MEAN:**

1. afflicted (p. 259)
2. twitter (p. 259)
3. puffed (p. 259)
4. scent (p. 259)
5. slanting (p. 259)
6. quarrel (p. 260)
7. cautiously (p. 260)
8. steep (p. 260)
9. overhung (p. 260)
10. cave (p. 260)
11. flame (p. 260)

12. alight (p. 260)
13. relief (p. 260)
14. preparations (p. 260)
15. shudder (p. 260)
16. immense (p. 260)
17. carving (p. 261)
18. chopper (p. 261)
19. tumbler (p. 261)
20. salt-cellar (p. 261)
21. recently (p. 262)
22. accustomed (p. 263)

23. perceived (p. 263)
24. sashes (p. 263)
25. mercy (p. 264)
26. incapable (p. 264)
27. midges (p. 265)
28. contained (p. 266)
29. addled (p. 266)
30. grubs (p. 266)
31. wantonly (p. 266)

✏️ **PLEASE ANSWER THESE IN COMPLETE SENTENCES:**

32. What information did Cottontail pass on to Peter and Benjamin?

33. What did the house look like where Tommy Brock was staying?

34. Where had he hidden the bunnies?

35. What was Tommy Brock doing when the rabbits got to the house?

36. How did the rabbits discover where the bunnies were hidden?

37. How did Benjamin, the dad, feel when he found out his children were still alive?

38. What did Benjamin and Peter decide to do to rescue the bunnies?

39. What did the rabbits do when they heard Mr. Tod coming?

40. In what kind of mood was the fox—and why?

✔ **LEARNING MORE:**

41. Which illustration from this part of the story is your favorite—and why?

42. Draw a picture of your favorite part of this section of the story.

43. Make up sentences using at least twelve of the vocabulary words.

The Tale of Mr. Tod

Part III

☐ **READ PAGES 266b-273a IN <u>The Tale of Mr. Tod</u>.**

❧ **FIND OUT WHAT THESE WORDS MEAN:**

1. fumed (p. 266)
2. persistently (p. 267)
3. plantation (p. 267)
4. bristled (p. 267)
5. odious (p. 267)
6. absorbed (p. 267)
7. walking-stick (p. 268)
8. coal-scuttle (p. 268)
9. incurably (p. 268)
10. indolent (p. 268)
11. undid (p. 269)
12. creaked (p. 269)
13. proceedings (p. 269)
14. peculiar (p. 269)
15. uneasy (p. 269)
16. conscientiously (p. 269)
17. coil (p. 270)
18. staggered (p. 270)
19. industriously (p. 270)
20. apoplectic (p. 270)

21. gingerly (p. 271)
22. mounted (p. 271)
23. head (p. 271)
24. bedstead (p. 271)
25. dangerously (p. 271)
26. tester (p. 271)
27. flapping (p. 271)
28. descended (p. 271)
29. intended (p. 271)
30. dangling (p. 271)
31. vindictive (p. 271)
32. considerable (p. 271)
33. slung (p. 271)
34. wobbling (p. 271)
35. ladled (p. 271)
36. by degrees (p. 272)
37. pendulum (p. 272)
38. preparations (p. 272)
39. strained (p. 272)
40. immensely (p. 273)

✎ **PLEASE ANSWER THESE IN COMPLETE SENTENCES:**

41. How did Mr. Tod feel when he looked into his kitchen and bedroom?
42. What was Tommy Brock doing that led Mr. Tod to believe he was fast asleep?
43. What clue does the author give us that Tommy Brock really wasn't asleep?
44. What was Mr. Tod's scheme to wake Tommy Brock?
45. What did Tommy Brock do right after Mr. Tod left the room?

✔ **LEARNING MORE:**

46. Which illustration from this part is your favorite—and why?
47. Draw a picture of your favorite part of this section of the story.
48. Make up sentences using at least twelve of the vocabulary words.

THE TALE OF MR. TOD

Part IV

❏ **READ PAGES 273b-280 IN <u>The Tale of Mr. Tod</u>.**

🍏 **FIND OUT WHAT THESE WORDS MEAN:**

1. obliged (p. 273)
2. gnaw (p. 273)
3. mystified (p. 274)
4. attentively (p. 274)
5. dinged in (p. 274)
6. caper (p. 275)
7. bold (p. 275)
8. disinfected (p. 275)
9. monkey soap (p. 275)
10. Persian (p. 275)
11. carbolic (p. 275)
12. sulphur (p. 275)
13. scalding (p. 275)
14. grappled (p. 276)

15. smashed (p. 276)
16. atoms (p. 276)
17. canisters (p. 277)
18. snarling (p. 277)
19. worrying (p. 277)
20. decidedly (p. 278)
21. reproaches (p. 278)
22. heavily (p. 278)
23. sulky (p. 278)
24. barricaded (p. 278)
25. triumph (p. 279)
26. recovered (p. 280)
27. dignity (p. 280)

✏ **PLEASE ANSWER THESE IN COMPLETE SENTENCES:**

28. How did Mr. Tod finally have to undo the rope—and how long did it take him?
29. What surprised Mr. Tod after the water fell onto the bed?
30. After Mr. Tod peered into the bedroom window and saw no movement, what did he think happened to Mr. Tommy Brock?
31. What surprise met Mr. Tod when he entered his kitchen?
32. What then happened between the fox and the badger?
33. What happened to the inside of the house as a result of the fox and badger's actions?
34. When did Benjamin and Peter come out of hiding?
35. Meanwhile, what had happened at Benjamin and Flopsy's home?
36. Why did Benjamin and Peter not need to hide after Benjamin rescued the baby bunnies?
37. How did Flopsy and Mr. Bouncer feel when Benjamin brought the bunnies home safely?
38. Did Flopsy and Benjamin forgive Mr. Bouncer?

✔ **LEARNING MORE:**

39. Which illustration from this part of the story is your favorite—and why?
40. Draw a picture of your favorite part of this section of the story.
41. Read this story to a younger child.
42. Make up sentences using at least twelve of the vocabulary words

THE TALE OF LITTLE PIG ROBINSON

Part I

☐ **READ PAGES 339-346a IN The <u>Tale of Little Pig Robinson</u>.**

❧ **FIND OUT WHAT THESE WORDS MEAN:**

1. quay (p. 341)
2. shallow (p. 341)
3. laden (p. 341)
4. rheumatics (p. 341)
5. ached (p. 341)
6. borrowed (p. 342)
7. plaid (p. 342)
8. top-knots (p. 342)
9. sure-footed (p. 343)
10. slimy (p. 344)
11. pitch (p. 344)
12. tide (p. 344)

13. vessels (p. 344)
14. grimy (p. 344)
15. colliers (p. 344)
16. scoops (p. 344)
17. ashore (p. 344)
18. cranes (p. 344)
19. stevedores (p. 344)
20. opportunity (p. 344)
21. cask (p. 344)
22. pulley (p. 344)
23. threaded (p. 345)
24. wheeling (p. 345)

25. hand-trucks (p. 345)
26. swooped (p. 345)
27. breakwater (p. 345)
28. blunt (p. 345)
29. shingle (p. 345)
30. spirits (p. 345)
31. mate (p. 345)
32. lads (p. 345)
33. commenced (p. 345)
34. dabbling (p. 346)
35. cinders (p. 346)

✎ **PLEASE ANSWER THESE IN COMPLETE SENTENCES:**

36. What was Susan, to whom did she belong, and what color was she?
37. Why did Susan do errands for Betsy?
38. What did Sam do?
39. What errand did Betsy ask Susan to do?
40. What one animal was not going to meet the boats—and why?
41. What color dress and shoes was Susan wearing?
42. How many steps did Susan need to climb down?
43. What did Susan see on the "Pound of Candles" that surprised her?
44. What was the name of Sam's boat?

✔ **LEARNING MORE:**

45. Learn more about seagulls. In the Reading section of your notebook, write about what you have learned.
46. Which illustration from this part of the story is your favorite—and why?
47. Draw a picture of your favorite part of this section of the story.
48. Make up sentences using at least twelve of the vocabulary words.

THE TALE OF LITTLE PIG ROBINSON

Part II

❑ **READ PAGES 346b-353a IN <u>The Tale of Little Pig Robinson</u>.**

🐛 **FIND OUT WHAT THESE WORDS MEAN:**

1. pound (p. 346)
2. note (p. 346)
3. Bong-tree (p. 347)
4. cosy, cozy (p. 347)
5. thatched (p. 347)
6. soil (p. 347)
7. cliffs (p. 347)
8. speckled (p. 347)
9. prosperous (p. 347)
10. peculiar (p. 347)
11. charming (p. 347)
12. squinted (p. 348)
13. clothes peg (p. 348)
14. drying (p. 348)
15. green (p. 348)
16. stiles (p. 348)
17. trodden (p. 348)
18. hedge (p. 348)
19. aggravating (p. 348)
20. tuppence (p. 349)
21. mend (p. 349)
22. venture (p. 349)
23. frock (p. 349)
24. knickers (p. 349)
25. instructed (p. 349)
26. gunpowder (p. 349)
27. pantechnicons (p. 349)
28. darning-wool (p. 350)
29. grunty (p. 351)
30. snappy (p. 351)
31. uneasy (p. 351)
32. tiresome (p. 351)
33. merry (p. 351)
34. larks (p. 351)
35. hoarse (p. 351)
36. rooks (p. 351)
37. strutted (p. 351)
38. motherly (p. 351)
39. ewe (p. 351)
40. catkins (p. 352)
41. primroses (p. 352)
42. moist (p. 352)
43. chestnut (p. 353)
44. greyhounds (p. 353)
45. bounding (p. 353)

✏️ **PLEASE ANSWER THESE IN COMPLETE SENTENCES:**

46. What were the names of Robinson's aunts?
47. Describe Little Pig Robinson.
48. What happened to the carrier man and his cart?
49. Name at least three of the seven things Robinson's aunt warned him about.
50. What were the six things that Aunts Dorcas and Porcas needed from the market?
51. What did Robinson see on his way through the fields?
52. What did Robinson plan to do with the primroses he picked?
53. With what did he tie them?
54. Whom did he meet on the road?

✔ **LEARNING MORE:**

55. Learn more about horses and donkeys. In the Reading section of your notebook, write about what you have learned.
56. Which illustration from this part is your favorite—and why?
57. Draw a picture of your favorite part of this section of the story.
58. Make up sentences using at least twelve of the vocabulary words.

THE TALE OF LITTLE PIG ROBINSON

Part III

❑ **READ PAGES 353b-362a IN <u>The Tale of Little Pig Robinson</u>.**

☙ FIND OUT WHAT THESE WORDS MEAN:

1. recently (p. 353)
2. flints (p. 353)
3. jolly (p. 353)
4. trust (p. 353)
5. sensibly (p. 353)
6. intelligence (p. 354)
7. shiny (p. 354)
8. girth (p. 354)
9. gaiters (p. 354)
10. parapet (p. 354)
11. sluggish (p. 354)
12. current (p. 354)
13. water-crowsfoot (p. 354)
14. rhubarb (p. 355)
15. rattle (p. 355)
16. roan (p. 355)

17. gaily (p. 355)
18. apprehension (p. 355)
19. native (p. 356)
20. vicious (p. 356)
21. brass (p. 356)
22. mingled (p. 356)
23. bordered (p. 356)
24. shunting (p. 356)
25. hooter (p. 356)
26. situated (p. 356)
27. headlands (p. 356)
28. straggling (p. 357)
29. suburb (p. 357)
30. inhabited (p. 357)
31. principally (p. 357)
32. shingle (p. 357)

33. whelk (p. 357)
34. marine (p. 357)
35. spyglasses (p. 357)
36. sou'westers (p. 357)
37. picturesque (p. 357)
38. panniers (p. 359)
39. creditably (p. 359)
40. bullocks (p. 359)
41. assisted (p. 359)
42. asparagus (p. 359)
43. bolted (p. 359)
44. alley (p. 359)
45. bellowing (p. 359)
46. courage (p. 359)
47. delays (p. 359)
48. airy (p. 359)

49. jostling (p. 359)
50. racket (p. 359)
51. cobble (p. 359)
52. hum (p. 360)
53. wares (p. 360)
54. trestles (p. 360)
55. periwinkles (p. 360)
56. jealousy (p. 360)
57. nibble (p. 360)
58. pewter (p. 360)
59. bustling (p. 360)
60. bow-pot (p. 360)
61. guaranteed (p. 361)
62. blushed (p. 361)
63. disentangling (p. 362)
64. responsible (p. 362)

✎ PLEASE ANSWER THESE IN COMPLETE SENTENCES:
65. What did Mr. Pepperil give to Robinson?
66. What was Robinson's cousin named?
67. When did Robinson feel apprehensive—and why?
68. Describe the town of Stymouth.
69. What did Robinson see in the roads of Stymouth?
70. What time was it when Robinson got to the market?
71. What did Robinson sell in the market?
72. What did Betsy buy from Robinson?
73. Who was helping Robinson find Mr. Mumby's store?

✔ LEARNING MORE:
74. Learn more about goats. In the Reading section of your notebook, write about what you have learned.
75. Which illustration from this part of the story is your favorite—and why?
76. Draw a picture of your favorite part of this section of the story.
77. Make up sentences using at least twelve of the vocabulary words.

THE TALE OF LITTLE PIG ROBINSON

Part IV

☐ **READ PAGES 362b-371a IN <u>The Tale of Little Pig Robinson</u>.**

🐛 **FIND OUT WHAT THESE WORDS MEAN:**

1. general (p. 362)
2. circumstance (p. 362)
3. approved (p. 362)
4. repulsively (p. 362)
5. feelingly (p. 362)
6. obtain (p. 363)
7. worsted (p. 363)
8. barley (p. 363)
9. patent (p. 363)
10. turnips (p. 364)
11. jumble (p. 364)
12. fingering (p. 364)
13. darning (p. 364)
14. helplessly (p. 364)
15. clip (p. 365)
16. rude (p. 366)
17. wistfully (p. 366)
18. vain (p. 366)
19. wagtails (p. 366)
20. sprained (p. 366)
21. tavern (p. 366)
22. patronized (p. 366)
23. siskin (p. 366)
24. stable (p. 366)
25. solitary (p. 367)
26. events (p. 367)
27. industrious (p. 367)
28. sprightly (p. 367)
29. tea-caddies (p. 367)
30. spotlessly (p. 367)
31. inns (p. 367)
32. frequented (p. 367)
33. seamen (p. 367)
34. lounging (p. 368)
35. jersey (p. 368)
36. fault (p. 368)
37. horn (p. 368)
38. outdone (p. 368)
39. alarming (p. 368)
40. ginger (p. 368)
41. tallow (p. 368)
42. lard (p. 368)
43. crackle (p. 368)
44. suspicious (p. 369)
45. basin (p. 369)
46. unbounded (p. 369)
47. amusement (p. 369)
48. rough (p. 369)
49. snarling (p. 369)
50. vessels (p. 369)
51. discharging (p. 369)
52. coasting (p. 369)
53. brig (p. 369)
54. bleat (p. 370)
55. pursers (p. 370)
56. hoisted (p. 370)
57. useful (p. 370)
58. superintending (p. 370)
59. schooner (p. 371)
60. decorated (p. 371)
61. significance (p. 371)
62. jetty (p. 371)
63. lapping (p. 371)
64. straining (p. 371)
65. hawsers (p. 371)
66. moored (p. 371)
67. stowing (p. 371)
68. direction (p. 371)
69. nautical (p. 371)
70. rasping (p. 371)
71. audible (p. 371)
72. tug (p. 371)

✏️ **PLEASE ANSWER THESE IN COMPLETE SENTENCES:**

74. Why did Robinson's Aunt Dorcas like Mr. Mumby's store?
75. What did the dog Tipkins ask Robinson?
76. What item on Robinson's list did Betsy help him obtain—and where?
77. How did Betsy know what color yarn Robinson needed?
78. Where did Betsy suggest Robinson leave his basket?
79. How did the two goldfinches feel about Robinson being at the market?
80. What did the stranger, the seaman, offer Robinson?
81. Is it wise to speak to strangers? Or even listen to them?
82. What did Robinson accept from and give to the stranger?
83. Where did Robinson let the sailor lead him?
84. Why did Robinson not like the name "Pound of Candles"?
85. Who was the first animal to spot Robinson with the seaman?
86. Why did Sam Ram not warn Robinson?
87. What was the captain's name on the "Pound of Candles"?

✔ **LEARNING MORE:**

88. Learn more about sheep and wool. In the Reading section of your notebook, write about what you have learned.
89. Which illustration from this part of the story is your favorite—and why?
90. Draw a picture of your favorite part of this section of the story.
91. Make up sentences using at least fifteen of the vocabulary words.

THE TALE OF LITTLE PIG ROBINSON

Part V

❑ **READ PAGES 371b-379a IN <u>The Tale of Little Pig Robinson</u>.**

🐛 **FIND OUT WHAT THESE WORDS MEAN:**

1. shaky (p. 371)
2. plank (p. 371)
3. blacking (p. 371)
4. rigging (p. 371)
5. descend (p. 372)
6. partake (p. 372)
7. muffins (p. 372)
8. crumpets (p. 372)
9. consumed (p. 372)
10. stool (p. 372)
11. lurch (p. 372)
12. bleach (p. 372)
13. tow rope (p. 372)
14. bows (p. 372)
15. master (p. 372)
16. heeled (p. 372)
17. tore (p. 372)
18. extremely (p. 373)
19. subsided (p. 373)
20. civil (p. 373)
21. contrary (p. 373)
22. fainted (p. 373)
23. ill-treated (p. 373)
24. petted (p. 373)
25. fretting (p. 373)
26. scampered (p. 373)
27. lazier (p. 374)
28. sour (p. 374)

29. disposition (p. 374)
30. maize (p. 374)
31. impropriety (p. 374)
32. greediness (p. 374)
33. disastrous (p. 374)
34. results (p. 374)
35. over-indulgence (p. 374)
36. mournful (p. 374)
37. foreboding (p. 374)
38. morose (p. 374)
39. gloomy (p. 374)
40. owl (p. 374)
41. neglected (p. 375)
42. duties (p. 375)
43. valeting (p. 375)
44. serenading (p. 375)
45. remonstrated (p. 375)
46. annually (p. 375)
47. sprouted (p. 375)
48. consequence (p. 375)
49. shoal (p. 375)
50. becalmed (p. 375)
51. strolled (p. 375)
52. boatswain (p. 375)
53. launch (p. 376)
54. contraption (p. 376)
55. davits (p. 376)
56. glassy (p. 376)

57. breath (p. 376)
58. absence (p. 376)
59. loin (p. 376)
60. sail cloth (p. 376)
61. appetite (p. 377)
62. siesta (p. 377)
63. proceed (p. 377)
64. crow's nest (p. 377)
65. telescope (p. 377)
66. latitude (p. 377)
67. longitude (p. 377)
68. archipelago (p. 377)
69. chart (p. 377)
70. compass (p. 377)
71. peremptory (p. 377)
72. contradicted (p. 377)
73. corns (p. 377)
74. proceeded (p. 378)
75. mends (p. 378)
76. port-hole (p. 378)
77. remained (p. 378)
78. watch (p. 378)
79. shivering (p. 378)
80. fashion (p. 378)
81. N.N.E. (p. 379)
82. shallow (p. 379)
83. scuttle (p. 379)
84. unselfish (p. 379)
85. grudge (p. 379)

 PLEASE ANSWER THESE IN COMPLETE SENTENCES:

86.   How did the seaman and Robinson cross from the shore to the ship?
87.   What animal did Robinson see aboard the ship—and what was he doing?
88.   What did Robinson eat in the ship's cabin?
89.   When he awoke, what did Robinson realize was happening?
90.   Sing the song that Robinson made up (p. 373).
91.   How many times did Robinson sing that song?
92.   How did he annoy the sailors?
93.   What could Robinson do aboard the ship?
94.   How did the cat treat Robinson?
95.   What did the sailors use for fishing bait?
96.   What did Robinson overhear the cook and another sailor talking about while he lay on the deck?
97.   Why did the two men cover him with sailcloth?
98.   What did the captain think was ahead?
99.   After the cat looked through the telescope, what did he report to the captain? Was it the truth?
100.   Why did he tell the captain there was not land ahead?
101.   What was the cat's plan for Robinson's escape?
102.   Who was supposed to be on watch that night?

✔ LEARNING MORE:

103.   Learn more about owls. In the Reading section of your notebook, write about what you have learned.
104.   Which illustration from this part of the story is your favorite—and why?
105.   Draw a picture of your favorite part of this section of the story.
106.   Make up sentences using at least fifteen of the vocabulary words.

THE TALE OF LITTLE PIG ROBINSON

Part VI

❑ **READ PAGES 379b-383 IN <u>The Tale of Little Pig Robinson</u>.**

🐛 **FIND OUT WHAT THESE WORDS MEAN:**

1. varied (p. 379)	15. shrieked (p. 381)	29. rig (p. 382)
2. assortment (p. 379)	16. brandishing (p. 381)	30. receded (p. 382)
3. necessaries (p. 379)	17. tugged (p. 381)	31. hull (p. 382)
4. fly papers (p. 379)	18. steadily (p. 381)	32. deck (p. 382)
5. gimlet (p. 379)	19. tropics (p. 381)	33. masts (p. 382)
6. hasty (p. 379)	20. phosphorescent (p. 381)	34. sandbank (p. 382)
7. farewell (p. 379)	21. horizon (p. 381)	35. fertile (p. 382)
8. ascended (p. 379)	22. ripple (p. 381)	36. silvery (p. 382)
9. suspended (p. 379)	23. uproar (p. 381)	37. strand (p. 382)
10. drowned (p. 380)	24. pursuit (p. 381)	38. oysters (p. 382)
11. placid (p. 380)	25. involuntarily (p. 381)	39. bread-fruit (p. 383)
12. delphinium (p. 380)	26. commenced (p. 381)	40. drawbacks (p. 383)
13. disputed (p. 380)	27. frantically (p. 381)	41. enthusiastically (p. 383)
14. trumps (p. 380)	28. exhaust (p. 382)	42. climate (p. 383)

✏️ **PLEASE ANSWER THESE IN COMPLETE SENTENCES:**

43. Why did the cat help Robinson?
44. What did the cat and pig pack aboard the escape boat as necessities?
45. How did the cat sabotage the other boats?
46. What did the sailors think the boat in the distance looked like?
47. Why did the sailors return in the boats to the "Pound of Candles" instead of following Robinson?
48. What did Robinson find on the island?
49. Who visited Robinson a year and a half later? What did they think of the island?
50. What other two animals visited Robinson?
51. What did Robinson continue to do?

✔ **LEARNING MORE:**

52. Learn more about ships and/or sailing. In the Reading section of your notebook, write about what you have learned.
53. Which illustration from this part is your favorite—and why?
54. Draw a picture of your favorite part of this section of the story.
55. Read this story to a younger child.
56. Make up sentences using at least twelve of the vocabulary words.

SUMMARY

PLEASE ANSWER THESE IN COMPLETE SENTENCES:

I. Of all the twenty-three books that you have read by Miss Beatrix Potter, name your top three favorites. List each title and why you especially liked each book.

II. Here is a list of some of the characters you have read about:

CHARACTERS

1. Tailor of Gloucester
2. Hunca Munca
3. Mrs. Josephine Rabbit
4. Ginger
5. Tom Thumb
6. Mr. McGregor
7. Squirrel Nutkin
8. Pig-wig
9. Tommy Brock
10. Mr. Jeremy Fisher
11. Susan the cat
12. Mr. Brown
13. Kep the collie
14. Mrs. Tiggy-winkle
15. Mr. Jackson
16. Johnny Town Mouse
17. Pig Robinson
18. Flopsy
19. Chippy Hackee
20. Samuel Whiskers
21. Thomasina Tittlemouse
22. Mr. Piperson
23. Ribby
24. Mr. Tod Fox
25. Mrs. Tabitha Twitchit

26. Mr. Benjamin Bouncer
27. Aunt Pettitoes
28. Cap't. Barnabas Butcher
29. Lucie
30. John Joiner
31. Dr. Maggotty
32. Stumpy the dog
33. Peter Rabbit
34. Mr. Piperson
35. Moppett and Mittens
36. Simpkin
37. Pickles
38. Mrs. Chippy Hackee
39. Anna Maria Whiskers
40. Benjamin Bunny
41. Goody Tiptoes
42. Simpkin
43. Timmy Willie
44. Tom Kitten
45. Miss Moppet
46. Jemima Puddle-duck
47. Mrs. McGregor
48. Pigling Bland
49. Fierce Bad Rabbit
50. Timmy Tiptoes

A. Of all the characters in all the books, which five did you like the best—and why?

B. Choose twenty of the characters listed and write their number and the letters from the character traits below that describe each of your list. (There will be more than one trait letter for each character number.) Example: 3. g,k,m,n [Mrs. Josephine Rabbit (3.) was industrious (g), organized (k), wise (m), and patient (n).]

CHARACTER TRAITS

a. helpful
b. cheerful
c. content
d. obedient
e. hospitable
f. alert
g. industrious
h. faithful
i. peaceful
j. creative
k. organized
l. trusting

m. wise
n. patient
o. generous
p. courageous
q. disobedient
r. selfish
s. mean
t. unpleasant
u. disorganized
v. dirty/messy
w. untruthful
x. foolish

C. For each of the books listed below, write the letter of the book and then numbers after it for each character that was a part of that story. (You may use the same character number more than once.)

A. The Tale of Peter Rabbit
B. The Tale of Two Bad Mice
C. The Tale of Tom Kitten
D. The Tale of Squirrel Nutkin
E. The Tale of Benjamin Bunny
F. The Tale of the Flopsy Bunnies
G. The Tale of Mrs. Tittlemouse
H. The Tale of Jemima Puddle-duck
I. The Tale of Mrs. Tiggy-winkle
J. Ginger and Pickles
K. Johnny Town-Mouse
L. The Tale of Timmy Tiptoes
M. The Pie and the Patty-pan
N. The Roly Poly Pudding
O. The Tailor of Gloucester
P. The Tale of Pigling Bland
Q. The Tale of Mr. Tod
R. The Tale of Little Pig Robinson

D. Write a story for each of three characters listed (of your choice) to tell what happened to them after the story ended, or of another adventure they had. Illustrate your stories.

III. Miss Potter was a naturalist (a person who studied God's creations) and an artist. Some other naturalist-artists have been:

Roger Tory Peterson

John James Audubon

Tasha Tudor

Ernest Thompson Seton

Learn more about at least two of these people and look at an example of their work. How does their style of drawing differ from Beatrix Potter's? In the Reading section of your notebook, write about what you have learned.

IV. Observe living things around you. Record what you learn. Draw pictures of them in a sketchbook, showing all the details you see. Remember to thank God for each creature—He made each special in its own ways. We are to always worship Him, the Creator, and never the creation. Colossians 1:16 in The Holy Bible says of Jesus Christ: "For by Him all things were created that are in heaven and that are on earth, visible and invisible..." He is very great!

SECTION II

WINNIE & CHARLOTTE

STUDY GUIDE:

A Guide for Children
for *Charlotte's Web,*
Winnie-the-Pooh,
and
The House At Pooh Corner

by Ann Ward

NOBLE PUBLISHING ASSOCIATES
GRESHAM, OREGON

A NOTE TO PARENTS

This Study Guide is designed to present an organized way to study three books: <u>Charlotte's Web</u> , <u>Winnie-the-Pooh</u> , and <u>The House At Pooh Corner</u>. It is hoped that it will help children to be exposed to some of the finest classics in children's literature.

These three stories teach about character qualities and friendship by watching how animals respond to situations. There are nice black-and-white line drawings in all three books.

Depending on the reading ability and dictionary skills of your child, you may want to go through the vocabulary lists with your child. Before having him/her begin using the Guide, make sure your child understands that a complete sentence is one complete thought. It begins with a capital letter and ends with a period (or ? or !). There is at least one naming word (pronoun or noun) and one action word (verb).

This Guide is meant to be "non-consumable" (not used up with each use; not written in). I suggest that you have your child begin a notebook section for this study - and have the answer sheets (answers written on notebook paper), drawings, and sheets with information on various topics of further study added to the notebook.

One of the activities for each book is to "read the story to a younger child." This will hopefully add more fluency in reading (after having learned the vocabulary words) - and allow your younger children to hear a good story.

Enjoy your child's visits with Charlotte, Fern, and Wilbur at the Zuckerman's farm and in the Hundred Acre Woods with Pooh, Christopher Robin, and all the rest.

Hopefully, this study will help your child gain an appreciation for excellent literature, a fine choice of words, and discernment about character traits.

Happy reading!

CHARLOTTE'S WEB

❑ READ PAGES 7-13 (Chapter I).

🍎 FIND OUT WHAT THESE WORDS MEAN:

1.	runt (p. 7)	13.	plaster (p. 9)	25.	nevertheless (p. 11)
2.	sneakers (p. 7)	14.	roller towel (p. 9)	26.	promptly (p. 11)
3.	sopping (p. 7)	15.	wobbled (p. 10)	27.	nursing (p. 11)
4.	sobbed (p. 7)	16.	untimely (p. 10)	28.	infant (p. 12)
5.	unfair (p. 7)	17.	armed (p. 10)	29.	appetite (p. 12)
6.	gently (p. 8)	18.	air rifle (p. 10)	30.	notice (p. 13)
7.	litter (p. 9)	19.	dagger (p. 10)	31.	blissful (p. 13)
8.	weakling (p. 9)	20.	guest (p. 10)	32.	entire (p. 13)
9.	injustice (p. 9)	21.	miserable (p. 10)	33.	charge (p. 13)
10.	queer (p. 9)	22.	specimen (p. 10)	34.	selecting (p. 13)
11.	carton (p. 9)	23.	distribute (p. 11)	35.	pupils (p. 13)
12.	damp (p. 9)	24.	early risers (p. 11)	36.	blushed (p. 13)

✏️ PLEASE ANSWER THESE IN COMPLETE SENTENCES:

37.   Who was the main character in the chapter? Tell several things about her.

38.   Where had Fern's father gone? What was he going to do - and why?

39.   How did Fern feel about this?

40.   What action did Fern take because of her feelings?

41.   What did Fern say to her father? In what tone of voice did she speak?

42.   According to The Holy Bible, how have we learned children are to speak to their parents? Was Fern being an example of this?

43.   What did Mr. Arable decide about the pig?

44.   What did Fern's father say to her about the pig?

45.   What did Fern do after looking at the little pig?

46.   Describe how the pig looked.

47.   Name all the members of the Arable family and tell at least one thing about each person.

48.   What did Mr. Arable tell Avery about getting a pig?

49.   How did Fern feed the pig?

50.   How did Fern feel about life that day?

51.   What name did Fern select for the little pig?

✔ LEARNING MORE:

52.   Learn more about farming and living on a farm. In the Reading section of your notebook, write about what you have learned.

53.   How could Fern have handled the situation of asking her father about the pig in a different way?

54.   Draw an illustration of your favorite part of this chapter.

55.   Read this section of the book to a younger child.

56.   Make up sentences using at least ten of the vocabulary words.

☐ READ PAGES 14 - 21 (Chapter II and part of Chapter III).

FIND OUT WHAT THESE WORDS MEAN:

1.	stroke (p. 14)	12.	journeys (p. 16)	24.	dressing (p. 19)
2.	bib (p. 14)	13.	wheel (p. 16)	25.	axle grease (p. 19)
3.	gaze (p. 14)	14.	tagged along (p. 16)	26.	loft (p. 19)
4.	adoring (p. 14)	15.	liking (p. 16)	27.	pitched (p. 19)
5.	complained (p. 14)	16.	brook (p. 17)	28.	stalls (p. 19)
6.	woodshed (p. 14)	17.	delightfully (p. 17)	29.	sheepfold (p. 19)
7.	apple-blossom (p. 14)	18.	oozy (p. 17)	30.	grindstones (p. 19)
		19.	provide (p. 18)	31.	monkey wrenches (p. 19-20)
8.	snout (p. 15)	20.	arranged (p. 18)		
9.	tunnel (p. 15)	21.	manure pile (p. 18)	32.	scythes (p. 20)
10.	enchanted (p. 15)	22.	perspiration (p. 19)	33.	swallows (p. 20)
11.	vanished (p. 16)	23.	harness (p. 19)	34.	milking stool (p. 20)
				35.	discarded (p. 20)

✎ PLEASE ANSWER THESE IN COMPLETE SENTENCES:

36.   Describe a typical day for Wilbur in his early days at the Arable's home.

37.   How did Wilbur stay warm in the box under the apple tree?

38.   What does the term "spring pig" mean?

39.   What did Fern's father tell her to do about Wilbur? Did she obey?

40.   Who purchased Wilbur?

41.   Describe all the different smells in the Zuckerman's barn.

42.   What do young pigs need?

43.   What other animals lived in the Zuckerman's barn?

44.   Why did the animals trust Fern?

45.   What were Mr. Zuckerman's rules for Fern while she visited Wilbur?

✔ LEARNING MORE:

46.   Draw an illustration of your favorite part of this chapter.

47.   Read this section of the book to a younger child.

48.   Make up sentences using at least ten of the vocabulary words.

☐ READ PAGES 22 - 30 (the rest of Chapter III).

❦ FIND OUT WHAT THESE WORDS MEAN:

1.	trough (p. 22)	9.	hired (p. 24)	18.	fuss (p. 27)
2.	chuckled (p. 23)	10.	slops (p. 25)	19.	comfort (p. 28)
3.	root (p. 23)	11.	pricked (p. 25)	20.	middlings (p. 28)
4.	sod (p. 23)	12.	fast (p. 25)	21.	popover (p. 28)
5.	prance (p. 23)	13.	dodge (p. 26)	22.	captivity (p. 29)
6.	twirled (p. 24)	14.	hind (p. 27)	23.	appealing (p. 29)
7.	cocker spaniel (p. 24)	15.	gander (p. 27)	24.	reconsider (p. 29)
		16.	dazed (p. 27)	25.	praise (p. 30)
8.	mending (p. 24)	17.	hullabaloo (p. 27)		

✐ PLEASE ANSWER THESE IN COMPLETE SENTENCES:

26.   How was Wilbur feeling one afternoon?

27.   Who visited him, and what did she suggest?

28.   How did Wilbur feel about being out of his yard?

29.   Where did Wilbur go, and what did he do?

30.   Who was Lurvy?

31.   How did Wilbur feel about being the center of attention?

32.   What did Wilbur wish would happen to comfort him?

33.   How old was Wilbur when he had this adventure?

✔ LEARNING MORE:

34.   Draw an illustration of your favorite part of this chapter.

35.   Read this section of the book to a younger child.

36.   Make up sentences using at least seven of the vocabulary words.

❏ READ PAGES 31 - 38 (Chapter IV).

❧ FIND OUT WHAT THESE WORDS MEAN:

1.	steadily (p. 31)	13.	skins (p. 32)	25.	twirling (p. 35)
2.	eaves (p. 31)	14.	morsel (p. 32)	26.	frolic (p. 35)
3.	courses (p. 31)	15.	marmalade (p. 32)	27.	merry (p. 35)
4.	lane (p. 31)	16.	gloomily (p. 33)	28.	sourly (p. 35)
5.	pigweed (p. 31)	17.	lonely (p. 33)	29.	gnawing (p. 35)
6.	spattered (p. 31)	18.	friendless (p. 33)	30.	spying (p. 35)
7.	gushing (p. 31)	19.	budge (p. 33)	31.	glutton (p. 36)
8.	downspouts (p. 31)	20.	mentioned (p. 33)	32.	stealthily (p. 36)
9.	occupation (p. 32)	21.	goslings (p. 34)	33.	crafty (p. 36)
10.	trench (p. 32)	22.	absolutely (p. 34)	34.	abroad (p. 36)
11.	hominy (p. 32)	23.	limit (p. 34)	35.	dejected (p. 36)
12.	prune (p. 32)	24.	slanting (p. 35)	36.	sulphur (p. 37)
				37.	thin (p. 37)

✏ PLEASE ANSWER THESE IN COMPLETE SENTENCES:

38.   What had Wilbur planned on the rainy day?

39.   Who was Templeton? Where did he live?

40.   How did Wilbur feel about the rainy day?

41.   What did Wilbur want?

42.   Who did Wilbur ask to play with him, and what were their responses?

43.   What did the voice say to Wilbur that evening?

✔ LEARNING MORE:

44.   Everyone feels sad sometimes. Name five things a person could do then.

45.   Draw an illustration of your favorite part of this chapter.

46.   Read this section of the book to a younger child.

47.   Make up sentences using at least ten of the vocabulary words.

☐ READ PAGES 39 - 48 (Chapter V).

❦ FIND OUT WHAT THESE WORDS MEAN:

1.	blackness (p. 39)	23.	spoil (p. 42)	43.	centipedes (p. 46)
2.	stirring (p. 39)	24.	objectionable	44.	crickets (p. 46)
3.	grain (p. 39)		(p. 42)	45.	trapper (p. 46)
4.	bin (p. 39)	25.	meekly (p. 42)	46.	miserable (p. 46)
5.	scraped (p. 39)	26.	salutation (p. 42)	47.	inheritance (p. 46)
6.	grinding (p. 39)	27.	whereabouts	48.	spinning (p. 47)
7.	property (p. 39)		(p. 43)	49.	pitch (p. 47)
8.	decent (p. 39)	28.	denying (p. 43)	50.	cruel (p. 47)
9.	motionless (p. 40)	29.	flashy (p. 43)	51.	intend (p. 47)
10.	weather-vane	30.	near-sighted (p. 44)	52.	argued (p. 47)
	(p. 40)	31.	blundered (p. 44)	53.	position (p. 47)
11.	gleam (p. 41)	32.	tangled (p. 44)	54.	wits (p. 47)
12.	thoroughly (p. 41)	33.	furiously (p. 44)	55.	sharp (p. 47)
13.	examined (p. 41)	34.	plunged (p. 45)	56.	clever (p. 47)
14.	stillness (p. 41)	35.	headfirst (p. 45)	57.	lest (p. 47)

Continued on next page.

15.	dawn (p. 41)	36.	silken (p. 45)	58.	numerous (p. 47)
16.	mysterious (p. 41)	37.	unwound (p. 45)	59.	suffering (p. 48)
17.	cleared (p. 41)	38.	detested (p. 45)	60.	mistaken (p. 48)
18.	party (p. 41)	39.	cockroaches (p. 46)	61.	exterior (p. 48)
19.	addressed (p. 41)	40.	gnats (p. 46)	62.	loyal (p. 48)
20.	appropriate (p. 41)	41.	midges (p. 46)		
21.	signal (p. 41)	42.	daddy longlegs		
22.	paused (p. 41)		(p. 46)		

✐ PLEASE ANSWER THESE IN COMPLETE SENTENCES:

63.   When did the author say it's hard to sleep?

64.   What did the voice say in the morning?

65.   What did this mean?

66.   What was the spider's whole name?

67.   Could Charlotte see Wilbur? Why or why not?

68.   What did Charlotte do to the fly - and why?

69.   How did Wilbur feel about what Charlotte did to other insects?

70.   What did Charlotte explain to Wilbur?

✔ LEARNING MORE:

71.   Read Proverbs 27: 14. Did the advice of the oldest sheep agree with what this says (see the second paragraph on page 42)?

72.   Read Ephesians 4: 29 - 32. What do you learn from this passage?

73.   Read I Samuel 16: 7. At what part of other people does the Lord want us to look? Did Wilbur do that at this point?

74.   Learn more about spiders and spider webs. In the Reading section of your notebook, write about what you have learned.

75.   Draw an illustration of your favorite part of this chapter.

76.   Read this section of the book to a younger child.

77.   Make up sentences using at least twelve of the vocabulary words.

☐ READ PAGES 49 - 55 (Chapter VI).

🍎 FIND OUT WHAT THESE WORDS MEAN:

1. fairest (p. 49)
2. fade (p. 49)
3. trouts (p. 49)
4. an equal (p. 49)
5. hitched (p. 49)
6. swathes (p. 49)
7. hoisted (p. 50)
8. timothy (p. 50)
9. jubilee (p. 50)
10. teeters (p. 50)

11. interlude (p. 50)
12. desperately (p. 51)
13. cramped (p. 51)
14. gratified (p. 51)
15. unremitting (p. 51)
16. effort (p. 51)
17. sincere (p. 51)
18. shamelessly (p. 51)
19. management (p. 52)
20. morals (p. 53)

21. conscience (p. 53)
22. scruples (p. 53)
23. consideration(p.53)
24. decency (p. 53)
25. compunctions (p. 53)
26. broad (p. 54)
27. disgust (p. 54)
28. appalled (p. 54)
29. ancient (p. 54)
30. untenable (p. 54)
31. lair (p. 54)

✏️ PLEASE ANSWER THESE IN COMPLETE SENTENCES:

32. Tell about some of the sights and activities of the farm in the summer time.

33. How did the goose know that the eggs would hatch the next day?

34. Who, after the goose, was the first to know of the goslings' birth?

35. How many eggs did the goose hatch?

36. What did the rat ask about the eighth egg?

37. Describe what kind of character the rat had.

✔ LEARNING MORE:

38. Learn more about geese. In the Reading section of your notebook, write about what you have learned.

39. Draw an illustration of your favorite part of this chapter.

40. Read this section of the book to a younger child.

41. Make up sentences using at least ten of the vocabulary words.

❏ **READ PAGES 56 - 62 (Chapters VII and VIII).**

🐛 **FIND OUT WHAT THESE WORDS MEAN:**

1.	campaign (p. 56)	7.	particularly (p. 56)	13.	conspiracy (p. 57)
2.	sensible (p. 56)	8.	victim (p. 56)	14.	hysterics (p. 59)
3.	pestering (p. 56)	9.	anaesthetic (p. 56)	15.	vaguely (p. 61)
4.	detested (p. 56)	10.	service (p. 56)	16.	low (p. 62)
5.	loathed (p. 56)	11.	fattening (p. 56)	17.	rambled (p. 62)
6.	screens (p. 56)	12.	rigid (p. 57)		

✏️ **PLEASE ANSWER THESE IN COMPLETE SENTENCES:**

18. How did the barn animals feel about flies?

19. What was the bad news that the old sheep had for Wilbur?

20. What did Charlotte do that calmed Wilbur?

21. How did Fern's mother feel about her spending so much time at the barn?

22. How did Fern's father feel about it?

✔ **LEARNING MORE:**

23. Draw an illustration of your favorite part of this chapter.

24. Read this section of the book to a younger child.

25. Make up sentences using at least five of the vocabulary words.

❏ **READ PAGES 63 - 70 (part of Chapter IX).**

🐛 **FIND OUT WHAT THESE WORDS MEAN:**

1.	boast (p. 63)	9.	dragline (p. 64)	17.	advise (p. 66)
2.	delicate (p. 63)	10.	sway (p. 65)	18.	lack (p. 66)
3.	rebuild (p. 63)	11.	oblige (p. 65)	19.	sedentary (p. 69)
4.	witnessed (p. 63)	12.	crouched (p. 65)	20.	struggles (p. 69)

Continued on next page.

5.	task (p. 63)	13.	stale (p. 65)	21.	delectable (p. 69)
6.	coach (p. 64)	14.	quitter (p. 66)	22.	bundle (p. 69)
7.	spinnerets (p. 64)	15.	summoning (p. 66)	23.	trill (p. 70)
8.	hurl (p. 64)	16.	thud (p. 66)		

✎ PLEASE ANSWER THESE IN COMPLETE SENTENCES:

24.   How many sections did Charlotte say each of her legs had?

25.   What did Wilbur boast?

26.   What did Wilbur use as a dragline? Did it work?

27.   What two things did Wilbur lack to build a web?

28.   What was Charlotte's opinion of the people's web (a bridge)?

29.   What did Wilbur say he'd rather be doing?

30.   Was the lamb's remark kind and building up or unkind and cutting down?

31.   How did the remark make Wilbur feel?

32.   What happened at about twilight time on the farm? How did these events make Fern and Wilbur feel?

✔ LEARNING MORE:

33.   Draw an illustration of your favorite part of this chapter.

34.   Read this section of the book to a younger child.

35.   Make up sentences using at least six of the vocabulary words.

☐ READ PAGES 71 -77 (rest of Chapter IX and part of Chapter X).

❦ FIND OUT WHAT THESE WORDS MEAN:

1.	troupe (p. 71)	6.	cool and collected	10.	determined (p. 74)
2.	pipers (p. 71)		(p. 71)	11.	gullible (p. 75)
3.	serious (p. 71)	7.	lightly (p. 71)	12.	mercy (p. 75)
4.	curiosity (p. 71)	8.	checked (p. 73)	13.	affectionately (p.75)
5.	trembling (p. 71)	9.	motionless (p. 74)	14.	strattled (p. 77)

✐ PLEASE ANSWER THESE IN COMPLETE SENTENCES:

15. How did Wilbur feel when he saw the goose and her babies?

16. What advice did Charlotte give Wilbur?

17. How did Charlotte feel about her promise?

18. What character quality did Charlotte have that enabled her to feel calm even though she didn't know how she was going to save Wilbur's life?

19. What did Charlotte say about the idea when it came?

20. What was special about Zuckerman's swing?

✔ LEARNING MORE:

21. Read Ecclesiastes 5: 5. How does God feel about keeping promises?

22. Draw an illustration of your favorite part of this chapter.

23. Read this section of the book to a younger child.

24. Make up sentences using at least seven of the vocabulary words.

☐ READ PAGES 78 - 84 (rest of Chapter X).

FIND OUT WHAT THESE WORDS MEAN:

1.	supporting (p. 78)	5.	gabbled (p. 82)	9.	drooling (p. 83)
2.	discouraged (p. 78)	6.	surly (p. 82)	10.	moodily (p. 83)
3.	gases (p. 80)	7.	perfumed (p. 82)	11.	bestirred (p. 83)
4.	scuttled (p. 80)	8.	dump (p. 82)	12.	descended (p. 84)
				13.	drowsed (p. 84)

✐ PLEASE ANSWER THESE IN COMPLETE SENTENCES:

14. What did Avery want to do to Charlotte?

15. What happened to Avery to stop him from proceeding from his plans?

16. What happened when the trough landed on the rotten goose egg?

17. What did Charlotte do while the other animals slept that night?

✔ LEARNING MORE:

18.   Draw an illustration of your favorite part of this chapter.

19.   Read this section of the book to a younger child.

20.   Make up sentences using at least five of the vocabulary words.

☐ READ PAGES 85 - 93 (Chapter XI).

FIND OUT WHAT THESE WORDS MEAN:

1.	pattern (p. 85)	6.	bewilderment	10.	gyromatic (p. 91)
2.	loveliness (p. 85)		(p. 87)	11.	transmissions (p. 91)
3.	veil (p. 85)	7.	miracle (p. 88)	12.	buggies (p. 92)
4.	exertions (p. 87)	8.	distinct (p. 88)	13.	buckboards (p. 92)
5.	solemnly (p. 87)	9.	notions (p. 90)	14.	principal (p. 92)
				15.	put up (p. 92)

✏ PLEASE ANSWER THESE IN COMPLETE SENTENCES:

16.   How did the rain affect the appearance of Charlotte's web?

17.   What did Lurvy see when he looked at Charlotte's web?

18.   How did this occurrence affect Lurvy - what did he do?

19.   How did Charlotte feel when she listened to the people talking?

20.   To whom did Mrs. Zuckerman give the credit?

21.   After he saw the spider's message again, what did Mr. Zuckerman say about Wilbur?

22.   Who did Mr. Zuckerman tell about the message after his wife?

23.   What changes occurred at the farm the next week?

✔ LEARNING MORE:

24.   In your opinion, were the changes that happened to the farm - and to the people on the Zuckerman's farm - good or bad?

25. Draw an illustration of your favorite part of this chapter.

26. Read this section of the book to a younger child.

27. Make up sentences using at least seven of the vocabulary words.

☐ READ PAGES 94 - 99 (Chapter XII).

❧ FIND OUT WHAT THESE WORDS MEAN:

1. roll (p. 94)
2. idiosyncrasy (p. 94)
3. proceed (p. 95)
4. terrific (p. 96)
5. particle (p. 96)
6. baser (p. 97)
7. directors' (p. 98)
8. source (p. 98)
9. supply (p. 98)
10. destiny (p. 98)
11. quivered (p. 98)
12. gruffly (p. 98)
13. adjourned (p. 99)
14. sweetly (p. 99)
15. sensational (p. 99)

✎ PLEASE ANSWER THESE IN COMPLETE SENTENCES:

16. What help did Charlotte ask of the other animals?

17. Who suggested the word "terrific"?

18. What help did the old sheep feel Templeton could give?

19. What did the sheep say to Templeton?

20. How did Charlotte answer Wilbur when he said he was not terrific?

✔ LEARNING MORE:

21. Read I Corinthians 10: 24. Which animals in the story did this well? Which looked only to their own interests?

22. Draw an illustration of your favorite part of this chapter.

23. Read this section of the book to a younger child.

24. Make up sentences using at least seven of the vocabulary words.

☐ READ PAGES 100 - 107 (part of Chapter XIII).

❦ FIND OUT WHAT THESE WORDS MEAN:

1. creatures (p. 100)
2. ripped (p. 100)
3. orb (p. 100)
4. radial (p. 100)
5. produce (p. 100)
6. foundation (p. 100)
7. snare (p. 100)
8. bright (p. 104)
9. crate (p. 104)
10. tattered (p. 105)
11. spikes (p. 105)
12. rummaging (p.105)
13. crumpled (p. 105)
14. noble (p. 106)
15. triumphantly (p. 107)

✐ PLEASE ANSWER THESE IN COMPLETE SENTENCES:

16. What are different types of spider thread like - and how are each used?

17. What kind of thread did Charlotte choose for the word "terrific"? Why?

18. What did Mr. Zuckerman tell Lurvy about Wilbur?

19. Why did Templeton like the dump?

20. How many times did Templeton need to go to the dump to get a word that Charlotte could use?

✔ LEARNING MORE:

21. Draw an illustration of your favorite part of this chapter.

22. Read this section of the book to a younger child.

23. Make up sentences using at least five of the vocabulary words.

❏ READ PAGES 108 - 112 (rest of Chapter XIII).

❦ FIND OUT WHAT THESE WORDS MEAN:

1. radiant (p. 108)
2. shone (p. 108)
3. writhing (p. 109)
4. affection (p. 109)
5. limit (p. 109)
6. romp (p. 109)
7. tangled (p. 110)
8. thrashing (p. 110)
9. wildly (p. 110)
10. tackle (p. 110)
11. sagging (p. 110)
12. mercilessly (p. 111)
13. lashed (p. 111)
14. midsection (p. 111)
15. budge (p. 111)
16. aeronaut (p. 111)
17. remarkable (p. 112)
18. lullaby (p. 112)
19. thrushes (p. 112)
20. rushes (p. 112)

✎ PLEASE ANSWER THESE IN COMPLETE SENTENCES:

21. Did Wilbur like the new straw to lay in?

22. What was the story that Charlotte told Wilbur about her cousin?

✔ LEARNING MORE:

23. How do you think telling about her cousin's persistence helped Charlotte?

24. Draw an illustration of your favorite part of this chapter.

25. Read this section of the book to a younger child.

26. Make up sentences using at least ten of the vocabulary words.

❑ READ PAGES 113 - 120 (Chapter XIV).

FIND OUT WHAT THESE WORDS MEAN:

1.	silently (p. 113)	6.	sociable (p. 115)	11.	regard (p. 118)
2.	sternly (p. 113)	7.	shifted (p. 117)	12.	fidgeted (p. 118)
3.	fascinating (p. 113)	8.	crochet (p. 117)	13.	incessant (p.118)
4.	fibs (p. 114)	9.	doily (p. 117)	14.	associate (p. 119)
5.	inventing (p. 114)	10.	knit (p. 117)	15.	offhand (p. 120)
				16.	relieved (p. 120)

✎ PLEASE ANSWER THESE IN COMPLETE SENTENCES:

17. What did Fern tell her mother while she helped with the dishes?

18. What was her mother's reaction?

19. What did Dr. Dorian say about a spider's web?

20. Who teaches spiders to spin a web?

21. What were Dr. Dorian's views about people talking?

22. What advice did Dr. Dorian give Mrs. Arable about Fern going to the barn?

✔ LEARNING MORE:

23.   Learn more about knitting and/or crocheting. In the Reading section of
        your notebook, write about what you have learned.

24.   Draw an illustration of your favorite part of this chapter.

25.   Read this section of the book to a younger child.

26.   Make up sentences using at least six of the vocabulary words.

☐ READ PAGES 121 - 128 (Chapter XV and part of Chapter XVI).

🐛 FIND OUT WHAT THESE WORDS MEAN:

1.   monotonous   9.   reputation (p. 122)   18.   egg sac (p. 124)
        (p. 121)   10.   glow (p. 122)   19.   versatile (p. 124)
2.   duty (p. 121)   11.   modest (p. 123)   20.   forsake (p. 125)
3.   warn (p. 121)   12.   fame (p. 123)   21.   Navajo (p. 126)
4.   rumor (p. 121)   13.   spoil (p. 123)   22.   lugged (p. 127)
5.   uneasy (p. 122)   14.   confident (p. 123)   23.   sponge bath (p. 127)
6.   anxiety (p. 122)   15.   satisfying (p. 123)
7.   attraction (p. 122) 16.   distinguish (p. 123)
8.   befriended (p. 122) 17.   inconvenient (p. 124)

✐ PLEASE ANSWER THESE IN COMPLETE SENTENCES:

24.   What did all the people and animals think of when they heard the crickets
        singing?

25.   How had "success" and people's attention affected Wilbur?

26.   What did Wilbur realize was one of the most important things in the world?

27.   Why did Wilbur hope to win some prize money at the County Fair?

28.   Why was Charlotte hesitant in promising Wilbur that she'd go to the Fair
        with him?

29.   How did the two families (the Arables and the Zuckermans) get ready on the
        morning of the Fair?

30.   What did Mrs. Zuckerman decide to do to Wilbur - and why?

✔ LEARNING MORE:

31.   Learn more about crickets. In the Reading section of your notebook, write about what you have learned.

32.   Draw an illustration of your favorite part of this chapter.

33.   Read this section of the book to a younger child.

34.   Make up sentences using at least ten of the vocabulary words.

☐ READ PAGES 129 -137 (rest of Chapter XVI).

🐛 FIND OUT WHAT THESE WORDS MEAN:

1.	cautiously (p. 129)	10.	conditions (p. 131)	19.	biffed (p. 133)
2.	trotters (p. 131)	11.	surpass (p. 131)	20.	cut (p. 133)
3.	pacers (p. 131)	12.	wildest (p. 131)	21.	contained (p. 133)
4.	trampled (p. 131)	13.	stowaways (p. 132)	22.	crouched (p. 135)
5.	foul (p. 131)	14.	tussle (p. 132)	23.	sunstroke (p. 135)
6.	remains (p. 131)	15.	pummeled (p. 133)	24.	jammed (p. 137)
7.	glaring (p. 131)	16.	buffeted (p. 133)	25.	sideboards (p. 137)
8.	veritable (p. 131)	17.	lacerated (p. 133)		
9.	gnawed (p. 131)	18.	scarred (p. 133)		

✏ PLEASE ANSWER THESE IN COMPLETE SENTENCES:

26.   What announcement did Charlotte make about the Fair?

27.   How did the oldest sheep help Charlotte in talking Templeton into going to the Fair?

28.   Did the people know that there were the two other animals in the crate?

29.   Describe how Wilbur's crate looked.

30.   What did Wilbur do when the men talked about killing him?

✔ LEARNING MORE:

31.   Draw an illustration of your favorite part of this chapter.

32.   Read this section of the book to a younger child.

33.   Make up sentences using at least ten of the vocabulary words.

❏ READ PAGES 138 - 145 (Chapter XVII).

🍎 FIND OUT WHAT THESE WORDS MEAN:

1. sprinkling (p. 138)
2. aloft (p. 138)
3. blatting (p. 138)
4. hearty (p. 142)
5. mildly (p. 143)
6. unattractive (p. 143)
7. personality (p. 143)
8. familiar (p. 143)
9. cracks (p. 143)
10. dislike (p. 143)
11. brief (p. 143)
12. interview (p. 143)
13. swollen (p. 144)
14. listless (p. 144)
15. poorly (p. 144)
16. wearily (p. 144)
17. fiercely (p. 145)

✏ PLEASE ANSWER THESE IN COMPLETE SENTENCES:

18. How much money did Mr. Arable give each of his children (see the top of page 139)?

19. This book was written nearly forty years ago. It was safer for children to do things by themselves than now. In what way do you think the parents' answer would be different now?

20. What did Mr. & Mrs. Zuckerman and Lurvy each want to see at the Fair?

21. What did Charlotte tell Wilbur about the pig in the next pen?

22. How was Charlotte feeling - and why?

23. How did the people use the hot blanket to help them stay cool?

✔ LEARNING MORE:

24. Draw an illustration of your favorite part of this chapter.

25. Read this section of the book to a younger child.

26. Make up sentences using at least seven of the vocabulary words.

❏ READ PAGES 146 - 151 (Chapter XVIII).

🍎 FIND OUT WHAT THESE WORDS MEAN:

1. keen (p. 146)
2. detected (p. 146)
3. crackle (p. 146)
4. wormy (p. 147)
5. clipping (p. 147)
6. humble (p. 148)
7. schemer (p. 148)
8. vanished (p. 148)
9. masterpiece (p. 151)

✐ **PLEASE ANSWER THESE IN COMPLETE SENTENCES:**

10.   What did Fern do in the evening?

11.   How did this affect her mother?

12.   What did Templeton do in the evening?

13.   Did Templeton do what Charlotte asked him to do?

14.   What word did Templeton bring back to Charlotte? What were its two meanings?

15.   What was Charlotte creating that evening?

✔ **LEARNING MORE:**

16.   Draw an illustration of your favorite part of this chapter.

17.   Read this section of the book to a younger child.

18.   Make up sentences using at least three of the vocabulary words.

▢ **READ PAGES 152 - 162 (Chapter XIX).**

🍂 **FIND OUT WHAT THESE WORDS MEAN:**

1.	shrunk (p. 152)	9.	waterproof (p. 153)	17.	licked (p. 156)
2.	curious (p. 152)	10.	attention (p. 154)	18.	hankering (p. 156)
3.	cocoon (p. 152)	11.	pep (p. 154)	19.	dopey (p. 157)
4.	nifty (p. 152)	12.	languishing (p. 154)	20.	suspiciously (p.157)
5.	magnum opus (p. 152)	13.	strand (p. 155)	21.	fluttered (p. 161)
6.	constructed (p. 153)	14.	feasting (p. 156)	22.	confetti (p. 161)
7.	guarantee (p. 153)	15.	carousing (p. 156)	23.	contented (p. 161)
8.	toughest (p. 153)	16.	gorge (p. 156)	24.	commotion(p. 162)
				25.	gazed (p. 162)

✐ **PLEASE ANSWER THESE IN COMPLETE SENTENCES:**

26.   What did Charlotte look like in the morning?

27.   Describe what was near her. Tell about some of its features.

28.   How many eggs did Charlotte lay during the night?

29.   What news did Templeton bring: a.) about the Fair from a rat's perspective, and b.) about the pig next to Wilbur?

30.   What did the Zuckermans do for Wilbur even though he hadn't won first prize?

31.   After Wilbur was cleaned, what was announced on the loud speaker?

✔ LEARNING MORE:

32.   What do you think the other farm animals were doing during Fair time?

33.   Draw an illustration of your favorite part of this chapter.

34.   Read this section of the book to a younger child.

35.   Make up sentences using at least ten of the vocabulary words.

☐ READ PAGES 163 - 170 (Chapter XX).

🍎 FIND OUT WHAT THESE WORDS MEAN:

1.   pompous (p. 163)
2.   extraordinary (p. 163)
3.   infield (p. 163)
4.   proceed (p. 163)
5.   disgust (p. 164)
6.   triumph (p. 165)
7.   distinguished (p. 165)
8.   sundry (p. 165)
9.   phenomenon (p. 165)
10.   analysis (p. 165)
11.   valuable (p. 166)
12.   governors (p. 166)
13.   bronze (p. 166)
14.   suitably (p. 166)
15.   engraved (p. 166)
16.   token (p. 166)
17.   complimentary (p. 167)
18.   collapsed (p. 167)
19.   blank (p. 167)
20.   unconscious(p.167)
21.   drenched (p. 169)
22.   ails (p. 169)
23.   grandstand (p. 170)

✏ PLEASE ANSWER THESE IN COMPLETE SENTENCES:

24.   What award did Wilbur earn - and why?

25.   What happened to Wilbur while the announcer was talking for a long time?

26.   What did Templeton do to help?

27.   How did each of the Arable and Zuckerman family members deal with being in front of the crowd of people?

✔ LEARNING MORE:

28. Draw an illustration of your favorite part of this chapter.

29. Read this section of the book to a younger child.

30. Make up sentences using at least seven of the vocabulary words.

❑ READ PAGES 171 - 175 (part of Chapter XXI).

❦ FIND OUT WHAT THESE WORDS MEAN:

1. strain (p. 171)
2. still (p. 171)
3. secure (p. 171)
4. recovered (p. 172)
5. emotion (p. 172)
6. deserve (p. 172)
7. wove (p. 172)
8. trifle (p. 172)
9. generous (p. 173)
10. sentiments (p. 173)
11. agony (p. 173)
12. racked (p. 173)
13. heaved (p. 173)
14. desolation (p. 173)
15. scene (p. 173)
16. thrashing (p. 173)
17. deserted (p. 174)
18. monkeyshine (p. 175)
19. accompany (p. 175)

✏ PLEASE ANSWER THESE IN COMPLETE SENTENCES:

20. How did Charlotte feel about Wilbur's success?

21. What did Charlotte say about Wilbur's future?

22. Why did Charlotte say she'd done the things she had for Wilbur?

23. What did Wilbur say to Charlotte?

24. Charlotte said something that made Wilbur feel very sad. What did she say - and why?

25. What did Wilbur make up his mind he must do?

26. How did Templeton respond to Wilbur's request for help?

✔ LEARNING MORE:

27. Draw an illustration of your favorite part of this chapter.

28. Read this section of the book to a younger child.

29. Make up sentences using at least ten of the vocabulary words.

❏ READ PAGES 176 - 179 (rest of Chapter XXI).

❦ FIND OUT WHAT THESE WORDS MEAN:

1.	wisecracks (p. 176)	5.	occurred (p. 176)	9.	drool (p. 179)
2.	snide (p. 176)	6.	desperate (p. 177)	10.	forlorn
3.	forepaws (p. 176)	7.	extreme (p. 178)		(p. 179)
4.	touching (p. 176)	8.	adrift (p. 178)		

✐ PLEASE ANSWER THESE IN COMPLETE SENTENCES:

11.   What did Wilbur promise Templeton when he was desperate to get Charlotte's egg sac?

12.   What did Templeton say about the egg sac?

13.   What was Wilbur's plan to transport the babies back to the farm?

14.   How did Wilbur say good-bye to Charlotte?

15.   Who was with Charlotte when she died?

16.   Did anyone know the large part Charlotte played in Wilbur's success? Did she receive lots of praise and recognition?

✔ LEARNING MORE:

17.   Draw an illustration of your favorite part of this chapter.

18.   Read this section of the book to a younger child.

19.   Make up sentences using at least five of the vocabulary words.

❏ READ PAGES 180 - 185 (part of Chapter XXII).

❦ FIND OUT WHAT THESE WORDS MEAN:

1.	lump (p. 181)	5.	bleak (p. 182)	10.	woodchuck (p. 183)
2.	affectionate (p. 181)	6.	lee (p. 182)	11.	untold (p. 183)
		7.	trinket (p. 182)	12.	satisfaction (p. 183)
3.	skillful (p. 181)	8.	keepsake (p. 182)	13.	chorus (p. 184)
4.	nipped (p. 181)	9.	gigantic (p. 183)	14.	ditches (p. 184)

✎ PLEASE ANSWER THESE IN COMPLETE SENTENCES:

15. How did Wilbur feel about returning home?

16. What things happened around the farm as the weather turned to autumn?

17. What did Fern say was the best thing in the world?

18. Did Wilbur keep his promise to Templeton? What was the result to Templeton?

19. What happened one spring morning? How did this make Wilbur feel?

✔ LEARNING MORE:

20. Draw an illustration of your favorite part of this chapter.

21. Read this section of the book to a younger child.

22. Make up sentences using at least four of the vocabulary words.

☐ READ PAGES 186 - 192 (rest of Chapter XXII).

FIND OUT WHAT THESE WORDS MEAN:

1.	BB shot (p. 186)	6.	brilliant (p. 191)	11.	admirers (p. 191)
2.	joy (p. 190)	7.	memory (p. 191)	12.	dull (p. 192)
3.	initial (p. 190)	8.	pledge (p. 191)	13.	garrulous (p. 192)
4.	daintily (p. 190)	9.	tranquil (p. 191)	14.	glory (p. 192)
5.	occasion (p. 190)	10.	housekeeping (p. 191)		

✎ PLEASE ANSWER THESE IN COMPLETE SENTENCES:

15. What happened to most all of the little spiders one warm spring day?

16. How did this make Wilbur feel?

17. Who had stayed behind in the barn? What were their names?

18. What did Wilbur tell the three spiders about Charlotte?

19. What did Wilbur and the spiders pledge to each other?

20. How did Wilbur feel about life?

✔ **LEARNING MORE:**

21.   Draw an illustration of your favorite part of this chapter.

22.   Read this section of the book to a younger child.

23.   Make up sentences using at least seven of the vocabulary words.

SUMMARY
CHARLOTTE'S WEB

✎ PLEASE ANSWER THESE IN COMPLETE SENTENCES:

I. Tell about your one or two favorite parts of the story.

II. Here is a list of some of the characters you have read about:

1. Fern
2. Wilbur
3. Charlotte
4. Templeton
5. the goose
6. the gander
7. the old sheep
8. Mr. John Arable
9. Mrs. Arable
10. Mr. Homer Zuckerman
11. Mrs. Edith Zuckerman
12. Lurvy
13. Avery Zuckerman

A. Of all the characters, which three did you like the best - and why?

B. Write a one or two sentence description about each of these characters.

C. Write the numbers of each of the characters and after them, list all the letters of the character traits that describe each character.
Character Traits:

a. helpful
b. cheerful
c. content
d. obedient
e. hospitable
f. alert
g. industrious
h. faithful
i. peaceful
j. creative
k. organized
l. trusting
m. wise
n. patient
o. generous
p. courageous
q. disobedient
r. selfish
s. mean
t. unpleasant
u. disorganized
v. dirty/messy
w. untruthful
x. foolish

D. Write a story for each of three characters listed (of your choice) to tell what happened to them after the story ended - or of another adventure they had. Illustrate your stories. Read them to a younger child.

III. Learn more about some aspect of farming or a specific type of farm animal.

IV. Learn more about what The Holy Bible says about friendship. Here are some of the many passages that tell us how to choose a friend and how to be a friend. Read the following passages and tell in your words what they say:

a. Proverbs 17: 17a
b. Matthew 7: 12
c. Colossians 3: 12, 13
d. Matthew 22: 39
e. Matthew 5: 7
f. Matthew 6: 34

V. Write at least five sentences about a good friend of yours. Tell what is special about him/her.

WINNIE-THE-POOH

☐ READ PAGES 3 - 9 (part of Chapter I).

❦ FIND OUT WHAT THESE WORDS MEAN:

1.	introduced (p. 3)	4.	admitted (p. 9)	7.	prickles (p. 9)
2.	growly (p. 5)	5.	slithered (p. 9)		
3.	head-over-heels (p. 9)	6.	gorse-bush (p. 9)		

✐ PLEASE ANSWER THESE IN COMPLETE SENTENCES:

8.   What was Edward Bear's other name?

9.   What relationship was Christopher Robin to the author?

10.   What did Winnie-the-Pooh hear from an oak tree in the forest?

11.   What is one special food that bears like to eat?

12.   What happened to Pooh in the tree?

✔ LEARNING MORE:

13.   Learn more about bears. In the Reading section of your notebook, write about what you have learned.

14.   Draw an illustration of your favorite part of this chapter.

15.   Read this section of the book to a younger child.

16.   Make up sentences using at least three of the vocabulary words.

☐ READ PAGES 10 - 16 (part of Chapter I).

❦ FIND OUT WHAT THESE WORDS MEAN:

1.	awed (p. 10)	5.	deceive (p. 13)	9.	deception (p. 16)
2.	daring (p. 10)	6.	gracefully (p. 14)	10.	pity (p. 16)
3.	deep (p. 12)	7.	level (p. 14)		
4.	relations (p. 12)	8.	suspect (p. 15)		

PLEASE ANSWER THESE IN COMPLETE SENTENCES:

11.   What did Winnie-the-Pooh ask Christopher Robin for - and why?

12.   What was Christopher Robin asked to do with the umbrella?

✔ LEARNING MORE:

13.   Learn more about clouds and rain. In the Reading section of your notebook, write about what you have learned.

14.   Draw an illustration of your favorite part of this chapter.

15.   Read this section of the book to a younger child.

16.   Make up sentences using at least four of the vocabulary words.

❑ READ PAGES 17 - 21 (rest of Chapter I).

🐝 FIND OUT WHAT THESE WORDS MEAN:

1.   verse (p. 17)   3.   sigh (p. 21)
2.   spoil (p. 18)   4.   trailing (p. 21)

✏ PLEASE ANSWER THESE IN COMPLETE SENTENCES:

5.   What did the bees do to the "cloud" in the sky?

6.   How did Winnie get down to the ground?

7.   Why did the man think Winnie-the-Pooh was called "Pooh"?

✔ LEARNING MORE:

8.   Learn more about bees.   In the Reading section of your notebook, write about what you have learned.

9.   Draw an illustration of your favorite part of this chapter.

10.   Read this section of the book to a younger child.

11.   Make up sentences using at least two of the vocabulary words.

☐ READ PAGES 22 - 29 (part of Chapter II).

❧ FIND OUT WHAT THESE WORDS MEAN:

1.   stoutness (p. 22)
2.   glass (p. 22)
3.   properly (p. 22)
4.   gaily (p. 24)
5.   sandy (p. 24)
6.   bank (p. 24)

7.   sudden (p. 24)
8.   scuffling (p. 24)
9.   silence (p. 24)
10.   bother (p. 24)
11.   condensed milk (p. 26)

12.   greedy (p. 26)
13.   sticky (p. 26)
14.   lovingly (p. 26)
15.   larder (p. 26)
16.   directly (p. 26)
17.   carelessly (p. 28)
18.   fetch (p. 29)

✎ PLEASE ANSWER THESE IN COMPLETE SENTENCES:

19.   Where was Rabbit's house?

20.   Did Rabbit want Pooh to visit him? How do you know that?

21.   What happened to Pooh when he tried to exit from Rabbit's home?

22.   What were the reasons Pooh and Rabbit each thought Pooh was stuck?

23.   Who did Rabbit go to get?

24.   What did Christopher Robin tell Pooh they'd have to do to get him unstuck?

✔ LEARNING MORE:

25.   Draw an illustration of your favorite part of this chapter.

26.   Read this section of the book to a younger child.

27.   Make up sentences using at least five of the vocabulary words.

☐ READ PAGES 30 - 33 (rest of Chapter II).

❧ FIND OUT WHAT THESE WORDS MEAN:

1.   sustaining (p. 30)
2.   wedged (p. 30)

3.   tightness (p. 30)
4.   slenderer (p. 31)

5.   cork (p. 32)
6.   nod (p. 33)

✎ PLEASE ANSWER THESE IN COMPLETE SENTENCES:

7.   What did Christopher Robin do for Pooh over the next week?

8.   How did Rabbit use Pooh's legs?

9.   How did Pooh finally get unwedged?

10.   What did Pooh do after he was free from being stuck?

✔ LEARNING MORE:

11.   Draw an illustration of your favorite part of this chapter.

12.   Read this section of the book to a younger child.

13.   Make up sentences using at least three of the vocabulary words.

▢ READ PAGES 34 - 43 (Chapter III).

❦ FIND OUT WHAT THESE WORDS MEAN:

1.	grand (p. 34)	6.	hostile (p. 38)	11.	muddled (p. 41)
2.	trespassers (p. 34)	7.	spinney (p. 38)	12.	shan't (p. 41)
3.	squeak (p. 36)	8.	larch (p. 38)	13.	particular (p. 41)
4.	puzzled (p. 38)	9.	intent (p. 40)	14.	deluded (p. 43)
5.	proceeding (p. 38)	10.	accidentally (p. 40)	15.	soothingly (p. 43)
				16.	brightened (p. 43)

✎ PLEASE ANSWER THESE IN COMPLETE SENTENCES:

17.   The sign that Piglet had near his home probably once said: "Trespassers Will Be Prosecuted." Look up "prosecuted" and tell what the sign might have meant.

18.   Tell the story of what happened to Pooh and Piglet as they were walking.

19.   Who was watching them all the time?

20.   When Piglet began to get more frightened, what excuse did he tell Pooh?

✔ LEARNING MORE:

21.   Draw an illustration of your favorite part of this chapter.

22.   Read this section of the book to a younger child.

23.   Make up sentences using at least five of the vocabulary words.

☐ READ PAGES 44 - 51 (part of Chapter IV).

❦ FIND OUT WHAT THESE WORDS MEAN:

1.	thistly (p. 44)	7.	heather (p. 48)	13.	customary (p. 50)
2.	stumping (p. 45)	8.	sandstone (p. 48)	14.	procedure (p. 50)
3.	gloomy (p. 45)	9.	old-world (p. 48)	15.	humbly (p. 50)
4.	manner (p. 45)	10.	charm (p. 48)	16.	issue (p. 50)
5.	copse (p. 47)	11.	delicate (p. 48)	17.	wistfully (p. 51)
6.	dowdy (p. 47)	12.	moping (p. 50)		

✐ PLEASE ANSWER THESE IN COMPLETE SENTENCES:

18.   What type of animal was Eeyore?

19.   What was Eeyore's problem one day?

20.   Tell about Eeyore's character - was he a cheerful animal?

21.   What did Pooh promise Eeyore?

22.   To whom did Pooh go for advice?

23.   What two things did Owl have before his front door?

24.   In what type of tree did Owl live?

25.   Which word was Owl saying which made Pooh think he was sneezing?

✔ LEARNING MORE:

26.   Draw an illustration of your favorite part of this chapter.

27.   Read this section of the book to a younger child.

28.   Make up sentences using at least ten of the vocabulary words.

❑ **READ PAGES 52 - 60 (rest of Chapter IV and part of Chapter V).**

🍎 **FIND OUT WHAT THESE WORDS MEAN:**

1. turn (p. 52)   3. frisked (p. 54)   6. cunning (p. 58)
2. attached (p. 54 -   4. lumping (p. 56)   7. pit (p. 58)
    two meanings)   5. edged (p. 57)   8. clever (p. 60)

✏️ **PLEASE ANSWER THESE IN COMPLETE SENTENCES:**

9.   Was Pooh really being a good listener to Owl?

10. What did Pooh notice about the bell-pull?

11. What did Eeyore do after his tail had been refastened?

12. Did Christopher Robin, Pooh, or Piglet really know what a Heffalump was?

13. How did Pooh and Piglet decide to trap a heffalump?

✔ **LEARNING MORE:**

14. Learn more about donkeys. In the Reading section of your notebook, write about what you have learned.

15. Draw an illustration of your favorite part of this chapter.

16. Read this section of the book to a younger child.

17. Make up sentences using at least three of the vocabulary words.

❑ **READ PAGES 61 - 71 (rest of Chapter V).**

🍎 **FIND OUT WHAT THESE WORDS MEAN:**

1. steal (p. 63)   4. miserably (p. 65)   7. jiggeting (p. 67)
2. sinking (p. 63)   5. half-light (p. 65)   8. despair (p. 69)
3. goloptious (p. 64)   6. polish (p. 66)   9. scampering (p.70)

✐ PLEASE ANSWER THESE IN COMPLETE SENTENCES:

1. What did Pooh and Piglet put in the bottom of the heffalump trap?

2. What happened to Pooh in the middle of the night?

3. How did Piglet feel when he saw the animal in the bottom of the trap?

4. What would you have done if you had found an animal in the trap?

5. What was Pooh doing while Piglet was going to Christopher Robin's house?

6. How did Christopher Robin feel about Pooh?

✔ LEARNING MORE:

7. Draw an illustration of your favorite part of this chapter.

8. Read this section of the book to a younger child.

9. Make up sentences using at least three of the vocabulary words.

▢ READ PAGES 72 - 79 (part of Chapter VI).

❧ FIND OUT WHAT THESE WORDS MEAN:

1.	pathetic (p. 72)	5.	mulberry (p. 74)	9.	breaking down (p. 77)
2.	crackling (p. 72)	6.	riddle (p. 74)	10.	proper (p. 77)
3.	bracken (p. 72)	7.	kindly (p. 75)	11.	miserable (p. 77)
4.	doubt (p. 72)	8.	returns (p. 76)		

✐ PLEASE ANSWER THESE IN COMPLETE SENTENCES:

12. Why was Eeyore feeling especially gloomy one day?

13. What did Pooh sing to try to cheer up Eeyore?

14. What did Pooh and Piglet decide to give to Eeyore?

✔ LEARNING MORE:

15.   Draw an illustration of your favorite part of this chapter.

16.   Read this section of the book to a younger child.

17.   Make up sentences using at least five of the vocabulary words.

❑ READ PAGES 80 - 89 (rest of Chapter VI).

❦ FIND OUT WHAT THESE WORDS MEAN:

1.   hoof (p. 85)   2.   sorrowfully (p. 88)

✐ PLEASE ANSWER THESE IN COMPLETE SENTENCES:

3.   What did Pooh decide to give to Eeyore when he realized he had eaten all the gift of honey?

4.   What did Pooh have Owl write on the pot?

5.   What happened to the gift that Piglet was going to give to Eeyore?

6.   What did Eeyore do with the two gifts that he received?

7.   What did Christopher Robin do for Eeyore on his birthday?

✔ LEARNING MORE:

8.   Draw an illustration of your favorite part of this chapter.

9.   Read this section of the book to a younger child.

10.   Make up sentences using at least one of the vocabulary words.

❑ READ PAGES 90 - 97 (part of Chapter VII).

❦ FIND OUT WHAT THESE WORDS MEAN:

1.   usual (p. 90)   3.   pluck (p. 94)   5.   disposition (p. 94)
2.   deprived (p. 94)   4.   affectionate (p. 94) 6.   huskily (p. 96)
                                                         7.   splendid (p. 97)

✏ PLEASE ANSWER THESE IN COMPLETE SENTENCES:

8.   How did Pooh, Piglet, and Rabbit feel about Kanga and Roo coming to their woods?

9.   What did they plan to do to Kanga and Roo?

✔ LEARNING MORE:

10.   Learn more about kangaroos. In the Reading section of your notebook, write about what you have learned.

11.   Draw an illustration of your favorite part of this chapter.

12.   Read this section of the book to a younger child.

13.   Make up sentences using at least two of the vocabulary words.

❑ READ PAGES 98 - 105 (part of Chapter VII).

❦ FIND OUT WHAT THESE WORDS MEAN:

1.   nudge (p. 100)   3.   indignant (p. 105)
2.   shuddered (p. 105)   4.   severely (p. 105)

✏ PLEASE ANSWER THESE IN COMPLETE SENTENCES:

5.   How did Rabbit, Piglet, and Pooh trick Kanga?

6.   How did Piglet feel about being in Kanga's pocket?

7.   What two thoughts did Kanga have when she discovered Piglet in her pocket?

8.   What did she tell Piglet (Roo) that he would have that evening?

9.   How was Kanga fooling Piglet?

✔ LEARNING MORE:

10.   Draw an illustration of your favorite part of this chapter.

11.   Read this section of the book to a younger child.

12.   Make up sentences using at least two of the vocabulary words.

❑ **READ PAGES 106 - 113 (rest of Chapter VII and part of Chapter VIII).**

❦ **FIND OUT WHAT THESE WORDS MEAN:**

1. firmly (p. 106)   3. flannel (p. 106)   5. expedition (p. 112)
2. lathery (p. 106)   4. spruced (p. 111)   6. provisions (p. 113)

✐ **PLEASE ANSWER THESE IN COMPLETE SENTENCES:**

7. What did Kanga do to Piglet after his bath?

8. Who came knocking on Kanga's door?

9. What name did Christopher Robin make up for Piglet?

10. What did Christopher Robin putting on his boots mean to Pooh?

11. What expedition were they going to go on that day?

✔ **LEARNING MORE:**

12. Learn more about the North Pole. In the Reading section of your notebook, write about what you have learned.

13. Draw an illustration of your favorite part of this chapter.

14. Read this section of the book to a younger child.

15. Make up sentences using at least two of the vocabulary words.

❑ **READ PAGES 114 - 121 (part of Chapter VIII).**

❦ **FIND OUT WHAT THESE WORDS MEAN:**

1. unsettling (p. 115)   3. ambush (p. 119)   5. halt (p. 120)
2. oblige (p. 115)   4. crossly (p. 120)   6. melancholy (p. 121)

✐ **PLEASE ANSWER THESE IN COMPLETE SENTENCES:**

7. Who all went on the expedition?

8. How did Eeyore feel about the trip?

✔ LEARNING MORE:

9.   Draw an illustration of your favorite part of this chapter.

10.   Read this section of the book to a younger child.

11.   Make up sentences using at least three of the vocabulary words.

☐ READ PAGES 122 - 129 (rest of Chapter VIII).

🍎 FIND OUT WHAT THESE WORDS MEAN:

1.	interesting (p. 123)	5.	grumbled (p. 123)	10.	mention (p. 127)
2.	anecdote (p. 123)	6.	temporary (p. 124)	11.	numbed (p. 127)
3.	encyclopedia (p. 123)	7.	immersion (p. 124)	12.	modestly (p. 128)
		8.	bubbling (p. 125)	13.	revive (p. 129)
4.	rhododendron (p. 123)	9.	scolded (p. 125)		

✏ PLEASE ANSWER THESE IN COMPLETE SENTENCES:

14.   What happened to Roo in the water?

15.   What were the reactions of each of the following to the emergency?
        a.   Kanga   d.   Piglet   g.   Pooh
        b.   Eeyore   e.   Christopher Robin
        c.   Owl   f.   Rabbit

16.   After Roo was rescued, what did Christopher Robin announce about Pooh?

17.   Meanwhile, what was Eeyore still doing?

18.   What kind action did Christopher Robin do for Eeyore?

✔ LEARNING MORE:

19.   Draw an illustration of your favorite part of this chapter.

20.   Read this section of the book to a younger child.

21.   Make up sentences using at least seven of the vocabulary words.

☐ READ PAGES 130 - 137 (part of Chapter IX).

FIND OUT WHAT THESE WORDS MEAN:

1. jolly (p. 130)   4. surrounded (p. 131)   7. desert (p. 133)
2. sprawled (p. 131)   5. burrowing (p. 131)   8. ached (p. 134)
3. entirely (p. 131)   6. miserable (p. 133)

✐ PLEASE ANSWER THESE IN COMPLETE SENTENCES:

9. How did Piglet feel about the emergency situation which he faced?

10. What did Piglet finally do to help himself?

11. With how many honey pots did Pooh escape to the branch?

12. When Pooh saw the bottle floating past him, what did he do?

✔ LEARNING MORE:

13. Learn more about floods. In the Reading section of your notebook, write about what you have learned.

14. Draw an illustration of your favorite part of this chapter.

15. Read this section of the book to a younger child.

16. Make up sentences using at least three of the vocabulary words.

☐ READ PAGES 138 - 146 (rest of Chapter IX).

FIND OUT WHAT THESE WORDS MEAN:

1. astride (p. 139)   4. atmospheric (p. 140)   7. dorsal (p. 143)
2. paddling (p. 139)   5. unprecedented (p. 140)   8. forthwith (p. 145)
3. vigorously (p. 139)   6. directly (p. 141)   9. jerk (p. 145)

✐ PLEASE ANSWER THESE IN COMPLETE SENTENCES:

10. Tell about what Pooh used for a boat and what he named it.

11. What was Pooh's idea to Christopher Robin for a boat for the two of them?

12.   What was the new boat named?

13.   How did Piglet feel about being rescued?

✔ LEARNING MORE:

14.   Draw an illustration of your favorite part of this chapter.

15.   Read this section of the book to a younger child.

16.   Make up sentences using at least three of the vocabulary words.

☐ READ PAGES 147 - 154 (part of Chapter X).

❦ FIND OUT WHAT THESE WORDS MEAN:

1.   scent (p. 147)   2.   trodden (p. 152)   3.   sulkily (p. 153)

✐ PLEASE ANSWER THESE IN COMPLETE SENTENCES:

4.   What message did Christopher Robin give Owl to pass along?

5.   How did Pooh respond?

6.   How did Eeyore respond?

7.   What had Christopher Robin prepared for the party?

✔ LEARNING MORE:

8.   Draw an illustration of your favorite part of this chapter.

9.   Read this section of the book to a younger child.

10.   Make up sentences using at least one of the vocabulary words.

☐ READ PAGES 155 - 161 (rest of Chapter X).

❧ FIND OUT WHAT THESE WORDS MEAN:

1.   reproachfully   2.   dolefully (p. 157)   4.   over-rated
     (p. 156)   3.   sternly (p. 158)   (p. 159)

✐ PLEASE ANSWER THESE IN COMPLETE SENTENCES:

5.   For whom did Eeyore think the party was?

6.   What gift did Christopher Robin give Pooh?

7.   Why do you suppose Eeyore spoke badly of the gift?

8.   What did Pooh and Piglet say they each thought of, first thing each day?

✔ LEARNING MORE:

9.   Draw an illustration of your favorite part of this chapter.

10.   Read this section of the book to a younger child.

11.   Make up sentences using at least one of the vocabulary words.

SUMMARY
WINNIE - THE - POOH

✎ **PLEASE ANSWER THESE IN COMPLETE SENTENCES:**

I.   Tell about your one or two favorite parts in the book.

II.   Here is a list of some of the characters you have read about:

1.	Christopher Robin	5.	Piglet
2.	Winnie-the-Pooh	6.	Kanga
3.	Owl	7.	Roo
4.	Rabbit	8.	Eeyore

A.   Of all the characters, which three did you like the best - and why?

B.   Write a one or two sentence description about each of the eight characters.

C.   Write the numbers of each of the characters and after them, list all
the letters of the character traits that describe each character.
<u>Character Traits:</u>

a.	helpful	i.	peaceful	q.	disobedient
b.	cheerful	j.	creative	r.	selfish
c.	content	k.	organized	s.	mean
d.	obedient	l.	trusting	t.	unpleasant
e.	hospitable	m.	wise	u.	disorganized
f.	alert	n.	patient	v.	dirty/messy
g.	industrious	o.	generous	w.	untruthful
h.	faithful	p.	courageous	x.	foolish

D.   Write a story for each of three characters listed (of your choice) to tell
what happened to them after the story ended - or of another adventure
they had. Illustrate your stories. Read them to a younger child.

THE HOUSE AT POOH CORNER

☐ READ PAGES 3 - 11 (part of Chapter I).

FIND OUT WHAT THESE WORDS MEAN:

1. muffler (p. 4)
2. smackerel (p. 5)
3. timidly (p. 6)
4. thumping (p. 9)

✐ PLEASE ANSWER THESE IN COMPLETE SENTENCES:

5. What did Pooh decide to do one snowy day?

6. What was the idea that Pooh told Piglet while they were on the gate?

7. Who visited Christopher Robin?

✔ LEARNING MORE:

8. Draw an illustration of your favorite part of this chapter.

9. Read this section of the book to a younger child.

10. Make up a sentence using at least one of the vocabulary words.

☐ READ PAGES 12 - 20 (rest of Chapter I).

❦ FIND OUT WHAT THESE WORDS MEAN:

1. stuffy (p. 12)
2. macintosh (p. 14)
3. bloodhound (p. 15)

✐ PLEASE ANSWER THESE IN COMPLETE SENTENCES:

4. What did Eeyore tell Christopher Robin about his house?

5. How did Eeyore think his house was moved to the other side of the forest?

6. Did Pooh and Piglet tell Christopher Robin about the misunderstanding?

✔ **LEARNING MORE:**

7.   Draw an illustration of your favorite part of this chapter.

8.   Read this section of the book to a younger child.

9.   Make up a sentence using at least one of the vocabulary words.

☐ **READ PAGES 21 - 28 (part of Chapter II).**

🍎 **FIND OUT WHAT THESE WORDS MEAN:**

1.   looking-glass (p. 24)   2.   regretful (p. 25)   3.   refined (p. 26)

✐ **PLEASE ANSWER THESE IN COMPLETE SENTENCES:**

4.   What noise did Pooh hear in the middle of the night?

5.   What did Pooh tell the strange animal?

6.   What did Tigger wrestle with from the table?

7.   What did Pooh serve Tigger in the morning? Did Tigger like it?

8.   What was Tigger's opinion about acorns?

✔ **LEARNING MORE:**

9.   Learn more about tigers. In the Reading section of your notebook, write about what you have learned.

10.   Draw an illustration of your favorite part of this chapter.

11.   Read this section of the book to a younger child.

12.   Make up a sentence using at least one of the vocabulary words.

☐ **READ PAGES 29 - 37 (rest of Chapter II).**

FIND OUT WHAT THESE WORDS MEAN:

1. stripy (p. 29)   3. shillings (p. 32)   5. malt (p. 36)
2. murmured (p. 32)   4. extract (p. 36)   6. chops (p. 37)

PLEASE ANSWER THESE IN COMPLETE SENTENCES:

7. What did Tigger think of thistles?

8. Had Tigger been boasting - saying he liked everything to eat and then not really having that be true?

9. What did Tigger finally eat that he liked?

10. From then on, where did Tigger live?

11. What was special about 11:00 to Winnie-the-Pooh?

12. How did Piglet feel about Tigger?

✔ LEARNING MORE:

13. Draw an illustration of your favorite part of this chapter.

14. Read this section of the book to a younger child.

15. Make up sentences using at least two of the vocabulary words.

 **READ PAGES 38 - 45 (part of Chapter III).**

FIND OUT WHAT THESE WORDS MEAN:

1. muddled (p. 38)   2. organize (p. 40)   3. search (p. 40)

PLEASE ANSWER THESE IN COMPLETE SENTENCES:

4. What was Pooh doing when someone knocked at the door?

5. What had Rabbit organized - and why?

6. Did Pooh really know what he was looking for?

7.   What happened to Pooh?

8.   Who did Pooh meet at the bottom of the pit?

✔ LEARNING MORE:

9.   Draw an illustration of your favorite part of this chapter.

10.   Read this section of the book to a younger child.

11.   Make up a sentence using at least one of the vocabulary words.

☐ READ PAGES 46 - 55 (rest of Chapter III).

🍎 FIND OUT WHAT THESE WORDS MEAN:

1.   twitched (p. 46)   3.   gloating (p. 46)   5.   unsettle (p. 47)
2.   upset (p. 46)   4.   admiringly (p. 46)

✏ PLEASE ANSWER THESE IN COMPLETE SENTENCES:

6.   What did Piglet dream happened to him?

7.   When Christopher Robin came to the side of the pit and spoke, did the conversation go along as Piglet had dreamt?

8.   What did Piglet see on Pooh's back?

9.   What was Small's whole name?

10.   What did Eeyore learn two days later?

✔ LEARNING MORE:

11.   Draw an illustration of your favorite part of this chapter.

12.   Read this section of the book to a younger child.

13.   Make up a sentence using at least one of the vocabulary words.

❏ **READ PAGES 56 - 63 (part of Chapter IV).**

🍎 **FIND OUT WHAT THESE WORDS MEAN:**

1. sensible (p. 58)   3. honeycomb (p. 60)   5. watercress (p. 62)
2. fawn (p. 59)   4. nasturtiums (p. 61)

✏ **PLEASE ANSWER THESE IN COMPLETE SENTENCES:**

6. What problem did Pooh have one morning in making a decision?

7. What was Piglet planting?

8. What were Roo and Tigger doing that day?

✔ **LEARNING MORE:**

9. Draw an illustration of your favorite part of this chapter.

10. Read this section of the book to a younger child.

11. Make up a sentence using at least one of the vocabulary words.

❏ **READ PAGES 64 - 73 (rest of Chapter IV).**

🍎 **FIND OUT WHAT THESE WORDS MEAN:**

1. clutch (p. 64)   3. tunic (p. 70)   5. braces (p. 70)
2. earnestly (p. 69)   4. agog (p. 70)   6. nervously (p. 73)

✏ **PLEASE ANSWER THESE IN COMPLETE SENTENCES:**

7. Was Tigger able to climb in trees as well as he said he could?

8. Who saw Tigger and Piglet up in the tree?

9. What did Pooh think it was? What is the word Pooh was really thinking of?

10. What did Pooh do with the watercress and malt sandwiches?

11.   What was Piglet's idea about getting the two down from the tree?

12.   Did he mean any harm in his suggestion?

13.   What was Christopher Robin's plan to get the two animals down?

14.   Did Roo get down successfully?

15.   What happened when Tigger jumped?

✔ LEARNING MORE:

16.   Draw an illustration of your favorite part of this chapter.

17.   Read this section of the book to a younger child.

18.   Make up sentences using at least two of the vocabulary words.

READ PAGES 74 - 81 (part of Chapter V).

❧ FIND OUT WHAT THESE WORDS MEAN:

1.	depended (p. 74)	4.	air (p. 76)	7.	fluff (p. 78)
2.	captain(ish) (p. 74)	5.	lark (p. 77)	8.	herbaceous (p. 81)
3.	respects (p. 76)	6.	shortly (p. 78)	9.	frankly (p. 81)

✐ PLEASE ANSWER THESE IN COMPLETE SENTENCES:

10.   How was Rabbit feeling one morning?

11.   How did Rabbit think Christopher Robin felt about him?

12.   In what way did Rabbit feel that he and owl were different from all the other animals in the woods?

13.   What did the notice Christopher Robin read say? (spell the words correctly, please)

14.   What did Owl and Rabbit think that Christopher Robin was doing?

✔ LEARNING MORE:

15. Draw an illustration of your favorite part of this chapter.

16. Read this section of the book to a younger child.

17. Make up sentences using at least three of the vocabulary words.

☐ READ PAGES 82 - 91 (rest of Chapter V).

❦ FIND OUT WHAT THESE WORDS MEAN:

1. primroses (p. 82)
2. turtle-doves (p. 82)
3. cooing (p. 82)
4. violets (p. 82)
5. gumming (p. 82)
6. skylark (p. 82)
7. dreamily (p. 83)
8. meekly (p. 83)
9. education (p. 88)
10. treads (p. 88)
11. to and fro (p. 88)
12. glorious (p. 88)
13. scornfully (p. 90)

✐ PLEASE ANSWER THESE IN COMPLETE SENTENCES:

14. What was Rabbit trying to learn?

15. How did Pooh say he made up the songs?

16. What was Piglet doing that morning?

17. What kind thing was Piglet going to do with what he gathered?

18. What did Eeyore have in front of him?

19. What did Eeyore say Christopher Robin was doing each day?

20. How did Eeyore react when Rabbit knew the letter "A"?

21. What was changed about the notice on Christopher Robin's door the next day?

✔ LEARNING MORE:

22. Draw an illustration of your favorite part of this chapter.

23. Read this section of the book to a younger child.

24. Make up sentences using at least seven of the vocabulary words.

☐ **READ PAGES 92 - 99 (part of Chapter VI).**

 **FIND OUT WHAT THESE WORDS MEAN:**

1. sparkle (p. 92)   4. mark (p. 95)   7. distress (p. 98)
2. track (p. 92)   5. dignified (p. 97)   8. coldly (p. 98)
3. outland (p. 92)   6. eddy (p. 97)   9. revolving (p. 98)
                                                10. wash (p. 99)

✎ **PLEASE ANSWER THESE IN COMPLETE SENTENCES:**

11. About what did Winnie the Pooh want to make up a poem?

12. How did the animals play "Poohsticks"?

13. What grey object did the animals see floating under the bridge one day?

14. What did Eeyore say about being in the river?

✔ **LEARNING MORE:**

15. Learn more about rivers. And, in the Reading section of your notebook, write about what you have learned.

16. Draw an illustration of your favorite part of this chapter.

17. Read this section of the book to a younger child.

18. Make up sentences using at least three of the vocabulary words.

☐ **READ PAGES 100 - 108 (rest of Chapter VI).**

 **FIND OUT WHAT THESE WORDS MEAN:**

1. hearty (p. 103)   2. mere (merest: p. 103)   3. gruffly (p. 104)

✎ **PLEASE ANSWER THESE IN COMPLETE SENTENCES:**

4. What happened after Pooh dropped the rock into the river?

5. How did Eeyore respond to the help?

6. Why did Eeyore say he entered the river?

7. What did Christopher Robin suggest they do?

8. What did Pooh say (on page 108) about people?

✔ LEARNING MORE:

9. Draw an illustration of your favorite part of this chapter.

10. Read this section of the book to a younger child.

11. Make up a sentence using at least one of the vocabulary words.

☐ READ PAGES 109 - 117 (part of Chapter VII).

🍎 FIND OUT WHAT THESE WORDS MEAN:

1.	drowsy (p. 109)	4.	undoubtably (p. 110)	7.	rapidity (p. 113)
2.	earnestly (p. 109)	5.	nudge (p. 110)	8.	misty (p. 114)
3.	extremely (p. 110)	6.	astonishing (p. 113)	9.	awkward (p. 115)
				10.	indignantly (p. 115)

✐ PLEASE ANSWER THESE IN COMPLETE SENTENCES:

11. What did Rabbit tell Pooh and Piglet he wanted to do to Tigger?

12. What was Rabbit's plan?

13. What was the weather like the day of taking Tigger exploring?

✔ LEARNING MORE:

14. Draw an illustration of your favorite part of this chapter.

15. Read this section of the book to a younger child.

16. Make up sentences using at least three of the vocabulary words.

☐ READ PAGES 118 - 127 (rest of Chapter VII).

🐝 FIND OUT WHAT THESE WORDS MEAN:

1.   sidled (p. 120)   2.   tearing (p. 126)   3. yapping (p. 126)

✏️ PLEASE ANSWER THESE IN COMPLETE SENTENCES:

4.   Was Rabbit able to admit that they were lost?

5.   Where had Tigger gone when the others didn't come with him?

6.   After Kanga asked where the others were, what did Tigger do?

7.   What was Pooh's idea to get away from the sand-pit?

8.   What did Pooh say was calling him home?

9.   Who did Pooh and Piglet see as they were walking?

10.   How do you think Christopher Robin felt when he saw Pooh and Piglet?

11.   How did Rabbit feel before and after he saw Tigger?

12.   How successful was Rabbit's plan?

✔️ LEARNING MORE:

13.   Draw an illustration of your favorite part of this chapter.

14.   Read this section of the book to a younger child.

15.   Make up a sentence using at least one of the vocabulary words.

📖 READ PAGES 128 - 136 (part of Chapter VIII).

🐝 FIND OUT WHAT THESE WORDS MEAN:

1.	buffeted (p. 130)	4.	gale (p. 133)	8.	slithered (p. 136)
2.	shuffled (p. 132)	5.	blusterous (p. 133)	9.	hearthrug (p. 136)
3.	lingering (lingeringly: p. 132)	6.	thawing (p. 133)	10.	feverishly (p. 136)
		7.	forenoon (p. 135)		

✏ PLEASE ANSWER THESE IN COMPLETE SENTENCES:

11. What did Pooh and Piglet decide to do one day?

12. What type of weather was it?

13. What day of the week was it?

14. They were timing their visits so the two of them could be where at tea time?

15. What type of day did Owl call it?

16. Tell the story of what happened inside Owl's tree house?

✔ LEARNING MORE:

17. Learn more about the wind. In the Reading section of your notebook, write about what you have learned.

18. Draw an illustration of your favorite part of this chapter.

19. Read this section of the book to a younger child.

20. Make up sentences using at least three of the vocabulary words.

📖 READ PAGES 137 - 145 (rest of Chapter VIII).

🐝 FIND OUT WHAT THESE WORDS MEAN:

1.	letter-box (p. 137)	4.	considering (p. 139)	7.	astute (p.142)
2.	disturbance (p. 138)	5.	attached (p. 139)	8.	respectful (p. 143)
3.	annoyed (p. 138)	6.	state (p. 139)	9.	ascent (p. 144)

✏ PLEASE ANSWER THESE IN COMPLETE SENTENCES:

10. In what position was Pooh after the crash?

11. What was his attitude about the situation?

12. What was Pooh's idea for escaping?

13.   How did Piglet feel about the idea?

14.   How did the plans go?

✔ LEARNING MORE:

15.   Learn more about treehouses. In the Reading section of your notebook, write about what you have learned.

16.   Draw an illustration of your favorite part of this chapter.

17.   Read this section of the book to a younger child.

18.   Make up sentences using at least five of the vocabulary words.

☐ READ PAGES 146 - 151 (part of Chapter IX).

🐛 FIND OUT WHAT THESE WORDS MEAN:

1.   occurred (p. 148)   3.   informed (p. 150)   5.   shyly (p. 151)
2.   gallant (p. 149)   4.   flashed (p. 150)

✏ PLEASE ANSWER THESE IN COMPLETE SENTENCES:

6.   What message did Pooh find under his door one morning?

7.   What did Rabbit tell Eeyore about his responsibility in being a friend?

8.   How did Eeyore respond to the suggestion?

9.   What news did Pooh have for Piglet?

✔ LEARNING MORE:

10.   Draw an illustration of your favorite part of this chapter.

11.   Read this section of the book to a younger child.

12.   Make up sentences using at least two of the vocabulary words.

❑ READ PAGES 152 - 161 (rest of Chapter IX).

FIND OUT WHAT THESE WORDS MEAN:

1.   glowed (p. 152)   2.   blinch (p. 153)   3.   sarcastic (p. 156)

✎ PLEASE ANSWER THESE IN COMPLETE SENTENCES:

4.   How did Piglet feel about Pooh's new song?

5.   Who did Pooh and Piglet find at Owl's house?

6.   What did Kanga think of Owl's housekeeping?

7.   What news did Eeyore have - and how did the results affect Piglet?

8.   What was Piglet's answer?

9.   What question did Christopher Robin ask Piglet?

10.   What hospitable thing did Pooh say?

✔ LEARNING MORE:

11.   Draw an illustration of your favorite part of this chapter.

12.   Read this section of the book to a younger child.

13.   Make up a sentence using at least one of the vocabulary words.

❑ READ PAGES 162 - 171 (part of Chapter X).

FIND OUT WHAT THESE WORDS MEAN:

1.   unexpected (p. 166)   2.   gratifying (p. 166)

✐ PLEASE ANSWER THESE IN COMPLETE SENTENCES:

3.   What did all the animals in the forest seem to know?

4.   What did Eeyore do?

5.   How do you think everyone was feeling?

✔ LEARNING MORE:

6.   Draw an illustration of your favorite part of this chapter.

7.   Read this section of the book to a younger child.

8.   Make up a sentence using at least one of the vocabulary words.

❑ READ PAGES 172 - 180 (rest of Chapter X).

❦ FIND OUT WHAT THESE WORDS MEAN:

1.   factors (p. 173)   2.   suction pump (p. 173 - 174)   3.   knights (p. 174)

✐ PLEASE ANSWER THESE IN COMPLETE SENTENCES:

4.   Tell about the talk Christopher Robin had with Pooh in the special place in the forest.

5.   What special thing did Christopher Robin do to Pooh?

6.   What feelings do you think Christopher Robin was having?

7.   What feelings do you think Pooh was having?

8.   Have you ever had to say good-bye to anything/anyone? Tell about it.

✔ LEARNING MORE:

9.   Draw an illustration of your favorite part of this chapter.

10.   Read this section of the book to a younger child.

11.   Make up a sentence using at least one of the vocabulary words.

SUMMARY

THE HOUSE AT POOH CORNER

PLEASE ANSWER THESE IN COMPLETE SENTENCES:

1.   Tell about your favorite one or two parts of the book.

2.   Write a story for each of three characters in the book to tell what happened to them after the story ended - or of another adventure they had. Illustrate your stories.

3.   Look back over the vocabulary words from <u>The House At Pooh Corner</u>. Tell what each means.

SUMMARY

THIS YEAR'S READING

<u>Part I.</u>
   A.   Look back over the books you've read this year. What do you feel you have learned from them?

   B.   What three - five characters do you admire most - and why?

<u>Part II.</u>
   A.   Look over the vocabulary lists from the books you've read. Tell the meanings of all the words numbered 1, 5, and 10 (or others your mom or dad tell you to remember).